The Gardener's Guide
to Growing
ORCHIDS

The Gardener's Guide to Growing
ORCHIDS

Wilma and Brian Rittershausen

David & Charles

NOTE

Throughout the book the time of year is given as a season to make the reference applicable to readers all over the world. In the northern hemisphere the seasons may be translated into months as follows:

Early winter	December	*Early spring*	March	*Early summer*	June	*Early autumn*	September
Midwinter	January	*Mid-spring*	April	*Midsummer*	July	*Mid-autumn*	October
Late winter	February	*Late spring*	May	*Late summer*	August	*Late autumn*	November

A DAVID & CHARLES BOOK

First published in 2001
First paperback edition 2004

Copyright © Brian and Wilma Rittershausen 2001, 2004

Brian and Wilma Rittershausen have asserted their right to be identified as authors of this work in accordance with the Copyright, Designs and Patents Act, 1988.

A catalogue record for this book is available from the British Library.

ISBN 0 7153 1940 X

Designed and edited by Jo Weeks
Illustrated by Coral Mula

Printed in China by SNP Leefung
for David & Charles
Brunel House   Newton Abbot   Devon

Visit our website at www.davidandcharles.co.uk

David & Charles books are available from all good bookshops; alternatively you can contact our Orderline on (0)1626 334555 or write to us at FREEPOST EX2110, David & Charles Direct, Newton Abbot, TQ12 4ZZ (no stamp required UK mainland).

page 1   *Phragmipedium* Don Wimber.

page 2   *Cirrhopetalum* Kalimpong.

page 3   *Mexicoa ghiesbrectiana*.

CONTENTS

1

AN INTRODUCTION TO ORCHIDS

In the twenty-first century the orchid is far better understood than it has been at any time in the past. Gone are the old fallacies that tropical orchids can only be grown in a greenhouse with great heat and special skills. Gone also is the belief that orchids are only within the reach of the wealthy. Many years ago, when importing these jewels of the virgin forests was a difficult and uncertain business and man-made hybrids were a rarity, this was certainly true. But, today, it is very much the reverse.

Anyone with a general awareness of flowers cannot fail to see that orchids stand apart. Among the most beautiful of flowering plants, they also belong to one of

Cymbidium devonianum is a miniature species from India. The two blotches on the lip are known locally as the 'cobra's eyes'.

the largest and most remarkable plant families in the world. It is not known for sure exactly how many natural species of orchids occur in the wild – estimates vary from 25,000 to 30,000. Whichever figure is taken, it is most impressive, and to this can be added the 100,000 or more hybrids that have been produced over the last 150 years.

FLOWERS

All orchid flowers conform to a predesigned basic style, and yet every species is different: there appears to be no end to the variety that has evolved over millions of years. Where most flowers contain separate female and male organs (the stigma and stamens), orchids produce a single, finger-like structure, called the column, which contains both the male and female parts. The tip of the column holds the pollen, hidden by a protective cap, the anther. The pollen is held in solid masses, the pollinia, which can number two, four or occasionally eight. Surrounding this central structure are three outer sepals and three petals. The sepals mostly resemble the petals, and have the same colouring and a similar shape. The third petal, the lip or labellum, is always distinct, sometimes being smaller than the petals, but more often much exaggerated in size, brightly coloured and of a different shape. It is a signal to passing insects, which are attracted by the promise of nectar, and forms the ideal platform for them to alight and effect pollination; they seldom find nectar, however.

Pollination

In their pollination techniques the orchids are truly remarkable, and go to great lengths to achieve cross-fertilization of their flowers.

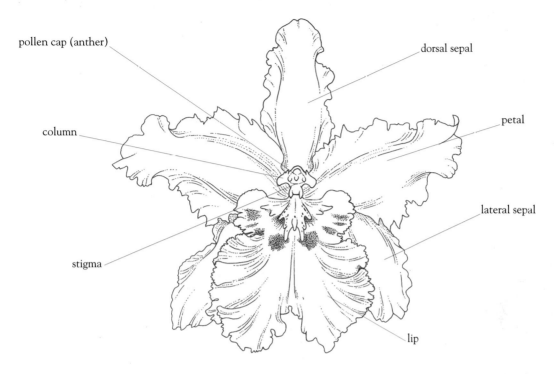

pollen cap (anther)

dorsal sepal

column

petal

lateral sepal

stigma

lip

A typical orchid flower will possess some features not generally found in other flowers.

Some depend upon mimicry to attract insects – a brilliant example is the European bee orchid, *Ophrys apifera*, the lip of which resembles a female bee. The orchids bloom at a crucial time, when the male bees emerge, but before the females make their appearance, usually about three weeks later. During this period, the bee, searching for a mate, encounters the orchid flower and alights on the lip, believing it has found the perfect partner. The orchid is designed not only to look like a female bee, but also to smell and feel like one. By the time the male discovers his error, if indeed he ever does, the pollen masses have become firmly attached to his head. He flies off to another flower and deposits the pollinia onto the stigma in a similar way. All species of *Ophrys* carry out similar deceptions.

Other orchids rely upon a strong fragrance to attract their specific insect. This may be the sweet perfume of nectar to attract bees or moths, or the less agreeable odour of rotting meat, which will bring forth carrion flies or wasps. For the same reason, some orchids produce their fragrance in the evening or early in the morning, timing its appearance to coincide with when

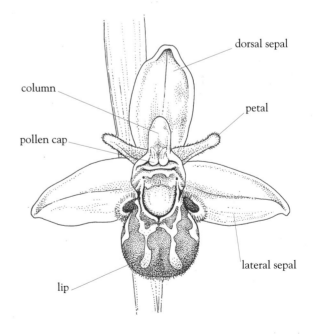

dorsal sepal

column

petal

pollen cap

lateral sepal

lip

In order to attract pollinating bees, the flower of the bee orchid, *Ophrys apifera*, is designed to look like a female bee.

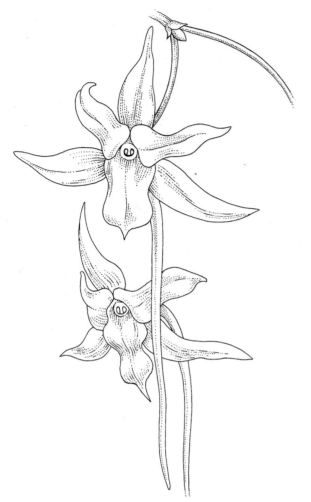

The nectar stored in the long spur of *Angraecum sesquipedale*, can only be reached by one species of moth.

releasing it unharmed. Another extreme example is seen in the amazing bucket orchid, *Coryanthes speciosa*. In this species, the lip forms an appendage – a 'bucket' – held below the flower. As it opens, the flower secretes an insect-attracting liquid to fill the bucket. Species of *Euglossa* bees are irresistibly attracted to the rim of the bucket. Where large numbers of bees collect, one inevitably falls into the liquid, and it is only by swimming to a funnel-like structure at one end of the bucket that it finds an escape route. In crawling out of the flower via this route, it presses against the column, taking the pollen with it.

Colour and shape

The diversity of form and variety of colour to be found among orchid flowers is unequalled by any other flowering plant. Every shade is represented, including black. Some of the blooms are so small as to need the assistance of a hand-lens to study their flora in any detail. Others may be as large as 20cm (8in) across. In one species, *Phragmipedium caudatum*, long, ribbon-like petals extend downwards to a length of over 60cm (2ft). If these petals were held horizontally, it would surely rank as the largest flower in the world!

Flowers can be long-lasting or very short-lived. Those of *Dendrobium atro-violaceum* remain in perfect condition for six or nine months, while a flowering head of *Epidendrum radicans* will provide a succession of flowers lasting for two years or more on a mature plant. *Sobralia macrantha*, on the other hand, produces a succession of exotic, paper-thin blooms whose short life will be just two days.

HABIT AND HABITAT

In their habits of growth orchids provide just as many surprises as in their blooms. Plants can be small enough to be comfortably contained in a thimble (*Pleurothallis grobii*), or twice the height of a man (*Grammatophyllum speciosum*).

Many genera produce pseudobulbs – swollen stems used for storage of water – joined by a creeping rhizome, for example cymbidiums, odontoglossums and dendrobiums. New pseudobulbs are added to the plant each year, producing what is called a sympodial type of growth. There are also orchids that, instead of a pseudobulb, have a vertical rhizome with new leaves appearing at the apex. These are known as the mono-

their particular pollinating insect is on the wing. The comet orchid, *Angraecum sesquipedale*, is an extraordinary example of this. The flower of this species has an elongated spur, over 30cm (12in) long, which is like a funnel at the back of the lip. When the orchid was discovered, it was suggested by Charles Darwin that a moth with a proboscis of the same length must visit this flower to pollinate it. The moth was discovered a considerable time later, long after his death, proving him correct.

A few orchids, such as *Porroglossum muscosum* (*Masdevallia muscosa*), have a highly sensitive, hinged lip, which will snap shut when agitated by the right-sized insect, trapping it to ensure pollination and then

Many orchids produce pseudobulbs, which are essentially swollen stems used for water storage.

the tree, and are therefore not parasitic, as once thought. Orchids and other epiphytes, such as bromeliads, merely take advantage of growing in the tree canopy where there is extra light and room for expansion. A few orchids grow in the same way upon mossy rocks and outcrops, and these are known as lithophytes. In cultivation they are grown in the same way as epiphytes.

Terrestrials

While the epiphytic way of life has been adopted by the majority of tropical orchids, it would not be possible in colder regions, where exposed roots could not survive. In these situations, orchids grow more conventionally in the ground, as terrestrials.

Terrestrial orchids can be found the world over, some of them managing with very little foliage, the main growth being a stalk where the leaves are small, and often close to the ground. One unconventional species from Australia, *Rhizanthella gardneri*, is known to exist

podials, and include phalaenopsis and vandas.

Orchids are found growing naturally on every continent in the world with the exception of the Arctic regions. But it is to the tropical counties that we look for the most exotic and beautiful forms. In their natural environment orchids can be divided generally into two types, epiphytes and terrestrials, although those in cultivation are mostly epiphytes.

Epiphytes

The epiphytes grow upon branches and trunks of trees. They adhere to the bark with thick roots that obtain all the nourishment they require from moisture that rises from the humid forest floor, as well as from rains and mists overhead. The plants also derive a weak form of fertilizer from bird droppings and other debris washed down the tree during heavy rain, and from the humus collecting in the axils of the branches, into which the roots will often penetrate. Epiphytes take nothing from

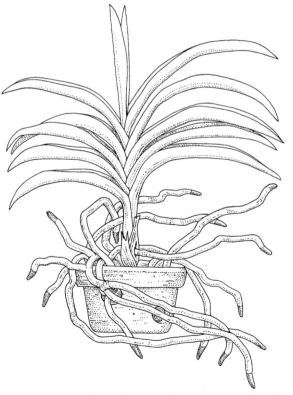

Monopodial orchids produce their leaves and their flowering spikes from a vertical rhizome.

entirely under the ground, with just the tips of the ant-pollinated flowers protruding above the surface. While such orchids are the exception, they illustrate the amazing extremes in this perplexing and intriguing family of plants.

A BRIEF HISTORY OF CULTIVATION

The credit for introducing tropical orchids into cultivation in Britain and elsewhere goes to the early Victorian horticulturists. Britain was at that time the main importer of tropical orchids and for many years led the world in cultural techniques. During the latter half of the nineteenth century, species were imported from the wild in their tens of thousands.

The long sea journeys and initial lack of knowledge meant that many of the imported orchids died. However, through perseverance, growers improved growing conditions, and special greenhouses and heating systems evolved to cater for the plants. Orchid growing became an obsession among the wealthy land-owning industrial barons of the day, and no country estate was complete without its collection of fabulous orchids. Competition was fierce among fanciers, and huge sums of money changed hands for the finest varieties.

Hybridizing

Although hybridizing was begun around the mid-1800s, the early breeders encountered many difficulties in the raising of seedlings. It was not until the early 1920s that the greatest advance in seed raising was achieved with the discovery of a method by which orchids could be raised artificially under sterile conditions, as opposed to the earlier, less successful method of sowing seed on the surface of the compost of a 'mother plant'. As a result of this new technique, many more seedlings survived, and the hybrids that were raised were the foundation stones for today's orchids. From the many thousands of species, only a very small minority have been used to create hybrids. These provide a much better prospect for the hobby-grower of today than do the rarer species, many of which are threatened in the wild, and are best conserved in specialist collections and botanical gardens.

Mass production

The latter part of the twentieth century heralded the introduction of mass-propagation through meristem culture, enabling one clone, or plant, to be produced in infinite numbers. This technique must be regarding as one of the great milestones in the history of orchids in cultivation. By it a further market opened up, giving the hobby-grower a choice of the finest hybrids at moderate prices. It has also created a mass-market for orchids as houseplants, and these can now be purchased in garden centres, major stores and other outlets, as well as the specialist nurseries, all of which confirms that orchids are easy plants to grow and are within everyone's reach.

ORCHID SOCIETIES

Socially, orchids have a great following; orchid societies have been founded all over the world. Their aims are to give genuine encouragement and advice to the beginner, and to share their interest with fellow enthusiasts. These societies organize their own shows and congresses, which are a great feature of the orchid year.

Dendrochilum latifolium produces a chain of creamy flowers with a pleasing fragrance.

2
WHERE TO GROW ORCHIDS

A greenhouse is one of the best places to grow orchids. Here, they can be given the combination of conditions they require – heat, light and water – all of which are equally important for their welfare. For example, it is of little use to maintain the right temperatures while allowing the plants to suffer from insufficient water. Maintaining the correct temperature is perhaps the most important and most expensive aspect of orchid growing. Should they be subjected to a single night of the greenhouse temperature falling below freezing, many of them will undoubtedly be killed. But should you fail to water or damp down for several days, no permanent harm will have been done, and any damage can be quickly rectified.

If you are not sure that you will always be able to tend your orchids on a daily basis, you can easily equip the greenhouse to be fully automatic so that it will take care of itself as far as possible.

GREENHOUSE DESIGN

The orchid greenhouse may consist of a single-span or double-span roof. It can be a modest lean-to or a conservatory. Orchids are very adaptable and more or less any type of structure can be converted for them, provided that adequate light, temperature and humidity can be given. An open site in the garden is best. Ideally it should be well away from large, overhanging trees, but at the same time taking advantage of any wall or hedge that may give some protection from the prevailing wind. If the structure is a conservatory, a southerly aspect will allow the maximum natural light and

Miltoniopsis are cool-house orchids. This is M. Maufant, a lovely modern hybrid of contrasting colours.

warmth from the winter sun. A northerly aspect can result in dark and cold conditions during the same period, which can add to the heating bill. Ideally, the greenhouse should run from north to south so that the sun passes over it and the plants inside can obtain the full benefit of the light.

Leave the floor of the greenhouse as earth, with just a strip of concrete or gravel for a central path. The walls up to staging level can be of brick or concrete blocks, and the sides and roof of the house framed in either timber or metal. There are various transparent plastic glazing materials that may be preferred to glass.

Build your greenhouse as big as possible. Small greenhouses are more subject to fluctuations in temperature, both in summer and winter, and, in summer, it is difficult to maintain any degree of humidity because the moisture is quickly lost due to the fact that the ventilators need to be wide open to keep the temperature down. Also, before long your orchid collection will outgrow its surroundings, and you will be faced with the problem of increasing the size of your greenhouse as it will always be unthinkable to dispose of any plants. No matter what size you build, always allow room to lengthen the greenhouse in the future.

Heating

The heating system should be completely reliable and it is a good idea to have an alternative to use in an emergency. Whatever type is chosen, it should be able to maintain the minimum temperature (see p.19) easily and at all times, without being overtaxed. It is less expensive in the long run to have several sources of heat spaced around the greenhouse, each giving off a gentle warmth and distributing the heat evenly, rather than one unit, working at a maximum capacity, to produce all the heat in one small area.

The most popular form of heating is electricity, usually from tubular bars or fan heaters. It can be easy to install and maintain and is completely labour-free when controlled by a thermostat. Fan heaters with a built-in thermostat are especially good as they circulate the air around the greenhouse, keeping a very even temperature. They should be positioned close to the floor so that the flow of air is not directed straight at any of the orchids. A fan heater will dry out the air more quickly, so you may need to damp down more frequently. To maintain humidity, it is a good idea to put a tray of water in front of the heater. Thermostatically controlled electric heaters can be more efficient than other forms of heating as they will not operate on days when the sun's warmth is sufficient.

Other suitable heating systems include gas- or oil-fired, automatic, thermostatically controlled boilers, with flow and return hot water piping. The boiler is installed outside the greenhouse with a tall chimney to take away all fumes clear from the building.

Heaters that burn paraffin or oil and stand inside the greenhouse can be extremely harmful to orchids because of the fumes they give off. They can cause bud-drop and other ailments in winter.

If your orchids are growing in a lean-to or conservatory built onto the side of the house, an extra radiator from the central heating system can be installed at little expense. Always keep at least two minimum/maximum thermometers in different positions so that a check can be kept on the lowest temperature recorded during the night.

Heat conservation

Conserving heat can be just as important as the actual heating of the greenhouse. With an older structure, all sources of draughts, such as holes, gaps in the glass or badly fitting doors and ventilators, should be attended to. Double glazing is a great asset for keeping up the temperature, particularly on cold, windy nights. It is usually included in the original construction of the greenhouse, an extra layer of glass or plastic being fixed to the inside, and should slide in and out quite easily so that it can be removed and cleaned in the spring. Cleaning is important as it will prevent a build-up of dirt and condensation in the cavity, which would reduce the light reaching the plants. Polythene sheeting or bubble plastic, which is lighter and cheaper to install, may also be used as a complete liner for the whole greenhouse. This will make a considerable difference by reducing draughts and increasing the temperature. Polythene soon becomes covered in condensation, however, so you need to fit it carefully, avoiding getting any creases or wrinkles which will cause drips. It will also quickly become discoloured and dirty, and is best replaced with new every year or two.

If you are going to divide the greenhouse into two or three sections to grow cool, intermediate and hot house orchids (see pp.18–19), use polythene or bubble pack plastic to make the divisions. A polythene curtain will save space and can be better than a door.

OTHER CONSIDERATIONS

Apart from location, design and heating, there are several other factors that will contribute to the greenhouse being suitable for growing orchids.

Staging

The staging needs to be at a height that allows your orchids to grow with sufficient headroom when in flower. A staging covered in gravel to retain moisture is fine; the orchids should be stood on upturned half-height pots. Alternatively, you can have a double staging, the top one, a few centimetres above, consisting of open slats. Both methods will allow a free movement of air around the plants. Add a lip to the edge of the top staging to prevent any small pots being knocked off the front, and place shelving at the back to create extra space.

Propagating frames

Even in the smallest greenhouse, it is worth making some provision for a simple propagating frame consisting of polythene sides and top with possibly a soil-warming cable laid on sand on the base. This can be most useful for starting back bulbs or small propagations or seedlings.

Water

Somewhere under the staging, out of the way, make room for a water butt. This can be connected by a pipe to the gutter outside for collecting rainwater so that you always have a store of water at greenhouse temperature. Make sure that the butt is positioned for easy dipping with a watering can.

Automatic sprinklers can be useful if you are away all day. When set to work at a certain temperature, they will keep the house moist and fresh on sunny days. Install the piping under the staging for damping down, and provide one rail above the plants for spraying the foliage.

Ventilation

The greenhouse should have top ventilators on both sides of the ridge, so that they may be opened on the leeward side to the prevailing wind. Here again, automation is the answer if you are away during the

Pleione speciosa is a spring-flowering orchid that needs to be grown very cool.

day. Bottom or side ventilators are useful, but not essential, although they can be a boon in extremely hot weather for keeping temperatures down (see also p.22).

One of the main problems with a small greenhouse is that in the winter valuable heat and humidity can be quickly lost through opening the ventilators to freshen the air. It is a good idea to install a small, inexpensive electric fan at one end of the greenhouse. Placed well above the plants under the ridgeboard, this can keep the air fresh, without the ventilators having to be opened. During the summer a fan will help to keep the orchids cool, and it can be sited so that it blows through the foliage without doing any harm.

Greenhouses that are designed specifically for orchids may have bottom ventilators situated below the staging. These are very advantageous in summer when they can be used in conjunction with the over-

PLATE I   *Coelogyne* species and hybrids

C. *swanniana*

C. Intermedia

C. *flaccida*

C. *fimbriata*

All flowers are shown at approximately half size

C. speciosa

C. cristata

One of the lady's slipper orchids, *Paphiopedilum* Sophromore is a very old hybrid that is still going strong.

head ventilators to cause a gentle current of fresh air to rise through the plants. In winter the bottom ventilators can be used on their own, in preference to the overhead ventilators, to avoid creating a draught. Unfortunately, most modern greenhouses do not have bottom ventilators: side ventilators, at staging level, are more common; they are too close to the plants, and so have limited use.

Shading

Shading is needed to keep the temperature down during hot weather. It can be provided in the form of white greenhouse shading paint, lath blinds or greenhouse netting, or a combination of all three.

Where lath blinds or plastic netting are used, put them on the outside of the glass, with a gap of about 20cm (8in) between the shading and the glass. This has the double benefit of shading the glass and allowing a cooling flow of air in between. There are various ways of attaching the shading to the outside glazing bars, depending upon whether your greenhouse is of wooden or metal structure – the manufacturers should be able to supply you with clips and fittings. Netting can either

be rolled onto the greenhouse roof, or made into panels, which are more easily handled.

Roller blinds or panels of netting are particularly useful during the spring, when they can be rolled up or taken down during dull, cloudy weather and replaced when the sun shines. If you are not around during the day, you can have automatically controlled blinds to work on their own depending upon the light intensity.

Netting or blinds inside the greenhouse are not a good idea for orchids. They will not cool the greenhouse in the same way, and may even increase the temperature in summer, when you are trying to reduce it during the day.

CREATING THE RIGHT CONDITIONS

Orchids are grown in three basic temperature ranges: cool, intermediate and hot (or warm). Which plants will grow in each section depends upon where they, or their ancestors, occurred in the wild. It is not wise to combine both cool and intermediate orchids in the same greenhouse, for example, unless separate areas are available for them. Cool-growing orchids that are kept warm to suit other inhabitants may fail to bloom because their growth is just too lush. Warmer-growing orchids that are kept too cold will not do well either, and their growth will slow up, also resulting in a lack of flowers. If a greenhouse is large enough, it may be possible to have one end kept cooler for those types that need it, while the other end is a few degrees higher to accommodate the warmer-growing types. Some will enjoy a combination of conditions; dendrobiums of the *D. nobile* type, for instance, will do well in the intermediate section during the summer while they are producing their season's growth, and can then be rested in the winter in the cool section.

THE COOL HOUSE

Most epiphytic orchids occur naturally in mountainous regions, many near the equator, but often as high as 2,500m (8,000ft) above sea level. At this elevation, they can experience violent extremes of temperature from extremely hot days to almost freezing nights, but owing to the rarity of the atmosphere, they thrive. In the greenhouse, all other conditions for their wellbeing can be imitated to suit the orchids, except the thin atmosphere, which cannot be reproduced. Nevertheless, these orchids will grow in a cool greenhouse where the night-time temperature is warmer than that of their natural environment. This factor means that orchids from different parts of the world can be grown together. Not all orchids that grow in a cool house come from high altitudes as do, for example, the odontoglossums, which inhabit the Andes throughout South and Central America. Many species from parts of Asia including China, Indonesia and India are found at lower elevations but still where temperatures are generally cooler. These include cymbidiums, bulbophyllums and a number of paphiopedilums. Australia also has its indigenous cool-growing species which are found in the temperate rain forests.

Around the end of summer, as the nights begin to get colder, the cool greenhouse needs to be heated. Heat will be required throughout the winter until late spring, when the outside temperature warms up sufficiently for the night-time temperature to be maintained by natural warmth. During the winter months, the minimum temperature should not be below 10°C (50°F), although on severe cold nights an occasional drop to 7°C (45°F) will not affect the plants, as long as they are kept on the dry side. Do not attempt to keep them at 7°C (45°F) every night, because this is too low for most plants to maintain their rate of winter growth, and they will then be slow to restart in the spring. During the day, the minimum temperature should rise by at least 6°C (10°F); this will occur naturally, and be much greater on sunny days.

During the summer, the night-time minimum will be easily maintained without any artificial heat, and cool summer nights are essential if the orchids are to bloom well. Again, the daytime temperature will rise naturally, and will vary from day to day, depending upon whether the sun shines or not. Shading and ventilation, as well as humidity, will help to control the daytime temperature, which should not be allowed to rise above 30°C (85°F). If it goes any higher, the plants will suffer from heat stress, which can be just as harmful to the orchids as cold nights in winter. There follows a guide to the temperature range to be aimed at throughout the year.

Winter day 16–18°C (60–65°F)
Winter night 9–10°C (48–50°F)
Summer day 16–30°C (60–85°F)
Summer night 10–11°C (50–52°F)

THE INTERMEDIATE AND HOT HOUSES

The cool greenhouse orchids are the most economical; however, if you have a greenhouse large enough to be divided into three sections, or even three separate greenhouses, you will be able to maintain the various temperature ranges to grow orchids that require cool, intermediate and hot conditions. In this way you can be sure of having some plants in flower all the year round.

Those orchids that grow naturally in the warmer climates are called subtropical. For these types, which include cattleyas, some dendrobiums, and paphiopedilums, an intermediate section is needed, while for the hotter-growing types, which include phalaenopsis, vandas and many more, even more warmth is required if they are to be grown well.

Because the intermediate house requires a higher temperature than the cool section, artificial heating is used for a longer period. In the same way, in the hot house it will be necessary to maintain the higher temperature by applying heat for almost the whole of the year. Once the hottest summer days have passed their peak, the night-time temperature will no longer be warm enough for these heat-loving plants, and some gentle artificial warmth will be needed.

The following guidelines are essential for intermediate and hot orchids.

Intermediate house
Winter day 16–18°C (60–65°F)
Winter night 13°C (55°F)
Summer day 21–30°C (70°–85°F)
Summer night 13–16°C (55–60°F)

Hot house
Winter day 21–24°C (70–75°F)
Winter night 16–18°C (60–65°F)
Summer day 24–30°C (75–85°F)
Summer night 16–18°C (60–65°F)

To balance these temperatures, keep a correspondingly high humidity. Damp down more frequently as the houses dry out more quickly. Well-gravelled staging and humidity trays filled with water will prevent total drying out. You will also need to take more care with ventilation. What can be a refreshing breeze in the

cool house may turn into a cold draught in the hot house. Orchids growing here will be more susceptible to chills, so it is a good idea to make it more draught-proof. Do not give less shade in an effort to increase the temperature through sunlight, however. Many warmer-growing orchids are just as shade-loving as the cooler types. The shading will help to maintain a more even temperature, and avoid rapid fluctuations.

During the summer months the orchids can be given considerable amounts of water, never allowing them to become completely dry at the roots. Feeding can be given at a slightly stronger measure than for the cool-growing orchids. Some of the warmer-growing types, such as dendrobiums, will need a resting period during the winter and throughout this time water is reduced or withheld altogether until they commence their new growth. During spells of severe wintry weather, when it is difficult to keep up the required temperature, the less water around the house the better; the orchids may be left on the dry side until conditions warm up.

HUMIDITY AND VENTILATION

Conditions inside any greenhouse – cool, intermediate or hot – are controlled by careful regulation of the humidity and ventilation, as well as by ensuring adequate shading during sunny weather.

Humidity

Humidity in the greenhouse should always balance the temperature. When the temperature is high, the humidity should be the same, to avoid conditions that are hot and dry. When the temperature is at its lowest, the humidity should also be less.

You can create a good humidity by damping down, a routine job carried out early in the day, when the temperature is rising. Soak the path and ground beneath the staging, as well as the staging itself. Mains water can be used, conserving rain water for the actual watering of the plants. All surfaces should be thoroughly wetted, not forgetting the back of the staging and areas that are out of sight. During the summer, when the light intensity is high and the plants are growing fast, they will benefit from as much moisture as you can give them in the atmosphere. On bright, sunny days spray

Previous page: *Phalaenopsis*, such as *P.* Cool Breeze, are heat-loving and should be grown in the hot house.

the plants overhead once or twice, making sure that the foliage has time to dry well before nightfall.

There are times, both during the summer and winter, when dull, sunless days will mean that the humidity remains naturally high, and damping down may be unnecessary for a day or two. On the other hand, during severe wintry weather, when bright, sunny days are followed by frosty nights, the temperature may fluctuate greatly and the amount of artificial heat required to keep it at its mimimum will cause the greenhouse to dry out more quickly, so extra damping may be necessary, particularly around the area close to the heater.

In the winter, damp down on a rising temperature, and not after midday, thus ensuring that all surplus moisture will have evaporated before nightfall, when the temperature drops. During spells of very cold weather, when the temperature may only rise by a few degrees above the minimum, allow the humidity to remain low, avoiding the conditions of cold and damp that will cause flowers to spot and, over a period, create black marks and other infections on the foliage. Persistent cold and damp conditions can weaken the plants, making them susceptible to virus disease.

Ventilation

Fresh air is important to orchids and should be provided whenever conditions permit. In the early part of the year, open the ventilators in the morning, after the damping down has been done. Do this a little at a time as the temperature rises. Depending upon the prevailing weather, ventilators may be left open until the afternoon. An electric fan will circulate the air, keeping the greenhouse fresh and buoyant, and avoiding any stagnation of the atmosphere.

During the height of the summer, it is possible to leave the ventilators fully open all day from early morning; during the hottest weather, in the cool house they can remain open all night as well. Keep a check on the temperature by having a minimum/maximum thermometer, which will record the minimum temperature inside the greenhouse during the night. Sometimes just a crack of ventilation overnight will assist in circulating the air. The extra air will cause faster drying out, so extra damping may be required to maintain some humidity.

Towards the end of the summer, the ventilators need to be closed down at night, and as autumn advances, shut them earlier in the day to conserve as much of the natural heat as possible. This will save you turning on the heater for a while longer.

There are fewer opportunities for opening the ventilators during the winter, but whenever possible, provide your orchids with fresh air for a short period, half an hour or so, when the temperature is well above the minimum. Open the ventilators just a little on the opposite side to the prevailing wind. Always avoid a cold draught getting onto the plants, and any sudden drops in temperature. If you are using an electric fan heater, this can be left on both day and night, and when you open the ventilators, it will prevent any drop in temperature.

Shading

During the summer months, after the greenhouse has been thoroughly damped down and fully ventilated, shading is the main factor in keeping the inside temperature down. To prevent it from becoming too high on sunny days, use a thick coat of white greenhouse shading paint to reflect much of the heat and reduce the temperature. If you are combining paint with lath blinds or greenhouse netting, a thinner coat will be sufficient.

As the summer heat wanes, gradually reduce the shading. First remove the blinds or netting; a little later wash off any remaining paint shading that has not been removed by the weather. During the winter, the orchids will benefit from as much light as possible, so it is a good idea to clean the glass, both inside and out, in the autumn.

Watch out for bright early spring sunshine. It is surprising how quickly the sun gains power, and it can cause dramatic increases in temperature on sunny days. Even when the outside weather is cold, temperatures inside the greenhouse can rise to summer levels in a just a few hours, and the bright sunshine can be particularly harmful to young growth and leaves, as well as to flowers. To prevent the foliage being scorched by any unexpected warmer conditions, apply a thin coat of shading early in the year. This can then be added to as necessary. If you collect your rainwater supply from the greenhouse roof, be sure to block up the drainpipe the first time it rains after putting on the paint shading. Some will be washed off, and you do not want the residue getting into the water tank. If you get caught out with a sudden burst of bright sunshine, place sheets of newspaper lightly over the leaves to protect them until you can get shading in place.

3

CULTIVATING AND PROPAGATING ORCHIDS

The following cultivation guidelines apply to all orchids, whether they are cool, intermediate or hot house types. Provided the right conditions are created for them, you will find the majority of orchids surprisingly easy to grow, and well-grown plants will reward you with a display of flowers in their season. Most problems that occur relating to orchids not blooming can be traced to incorrect culture.

WATERING

Epiphytic orchids dislike the extremes of being cold and wet or hot and dry. During the winter, many of them are resting and require very little water. While they are growing, they can be given much more moisture: the active roots will absorb copious amounts of water to enable them to develop their pseudobulbs. Watering little and often is not good for orchids – give one good, thorough soaking and no more until the compost is partially dry again. Try to avoid getting the compost so wet that it becomes sodden. A well-drained compost will allow air and water to filter freely through the pot, at the same time allowing sufficient moisture to be retained for the plant.

For best results, water your orchids with either a spouted can, using rainwater at greenhouse temperature, or a lance on the end of a hose using mains water. Apply water at the rim of the pot until the whole surface is thoroughly flooded. This will disappear within seconds so you can flood it again if necessary. Water that lingers on the surface of the compost, forming a puddle, is usually an indication either that the compost

Miltonioides laevis has fragrant flowers with striped brown petals and sepals and a bicoloured lip.

was far too dry due to underwatering, or that the compost has become clogged. This could be because of deterioration – if the plant has not been repotted for a long time, the compost will have decomposed – or the pot may be so full of roots that the water cannot penetrate, which can lead to underwatering.

Dip orchids growing in hanging baskets in the water tub. If necessary, you can leave them there until the compost stops bubbling. Do not do this with newly repotted plants, however, because the compost will simply float away: these plants are better watered with a rosed can. Orchids attached to pieces of wood with long aerial roots hanging down can be difficult to move, especially where these roots have attached themselves to their surrounding. Keep these plants wet by constant spraying, providing enough to soak the whole plant and its roots. Orchids like this will also absorb much of their moisture from the atmosphere in between being sprayed.

Water your orchids early in the day, when the temperature is rising, and preferably on a sunny morning. This is more important during the winter, when surface water will take longer to dry up: it is best to have all surplus water evaporated before dusk. An orchid that is actively growing needs watering when the compost is drying out, but before it becomes bone dry. Feel the compost or lift the pot to judge its dryness. If you are in doubt, leave it for another day.

A factor that influences how often you water a particular plant is its size in relation to its pot. A small plant, recently repotted into a larger size of pot, may need water once a week, while a large, pot-bound plant in a pot that has become too small, will want watering far more often, perhaps two or three times a week. It also depends upon the time of year: plants will dry out much more quickly in the summer than in the winter.

Underwatering happens when a plant is left dry for too long a period while it is actively growing. This will result in slowing of growth, the pseudobulbs will shrivel and the foliage become limp. Once a plant has deteriorated into this state, it can be difficult to get it completely wet again through watering in the normal way. In this case, put the pot in a bucket, fill the bucket with water to just below the rim of the pot (to avoid the compost floating away), and allow the plant to soak for half an hour or so. If the underwatered plant is pot-

bound, it may be best to repot it straight away, and this will give it a fresh start. After repotting, spray the foliage often to prevent further moisture loss through the leaves until the new roots get under way. With more attention to the watering from now on, the roots will be encouraged to grow and within a few weeks or months, the plant will gradually plump up and be able to continue its growing cycle. Orchids are always slow to react to poor conditions, at the same time being slow to recover from mistreatment. It can sometimes take years to bring a plant back into good health.

Overwatering, perhaps caused by the plant standing beneath a drip from a leaking greenhouse roof, will make the compost deteriorate and become sour, with the loss of the roots. Remove it from its pot and you will

A modern hybrid from Taiwan, *Phalaenopsis* Brother Golden Potential has spotted, yellow flowers.

Cymbidium Red Beauty × Gorey, like all cymbidiums, needs plenty of water during the summer and overhead spraying.

see that they are dead, blackened and full of water. Its top growth will resemble an underwatered plant: the loss of roots leads to the pseudobulbs shrivelling as they are no longer getting moisture. It may also have prematurely shed much of its foliage, resulting in a surplus of leafless pseudobulbs.

To save an overwatered plant, cut off the leafless pseudobulbs, retaining just two or three leading ones, which should have some leaves left. Remove the dead roots by cutting close to the base, leaving just sufficient to anchor the plant in a new pot, which will be smaller than the one from which you have taken it. Most plants will recover, but it can take a few years before new pseudobulbs, which are capable of flowering, develop.

RESTING

Epiphytes growing in the wild are subjected to daily downpours of heavy rain during the monsoon season, which is the growing period of these orchids. At other times of the year, they have to contend with long periods of drought. During the drought, growth ceases and a percentage of foliage is shed as the roots stop growing. The plant is now dormant and at rest. Extra light filtering through the tree canopy ripens the pseudobulbs and will encourage their flowering. The plants rely upon the large reserves stored in the pseudobulbs to produce their flowers, which in many species occurs before new growth starts.

With the exception of young seedlings and propagations, which should be kept continuously growing without any checks to their growth, most orchids in cultivation need some degree of rest, which may vary from a few weeks to several months. However, only plants that can be seen to be inactive should be rested. Any that are producing new growth or leaves need to be kept growing, and watering is continued as normal.

In the northern hemisphere, winter corresponds with the natural resting period. Therefore, in the autumn, when growth is completed and the pseudobulbs are plump and firm, they are ready to begin their rest. Many of the species can now be moved to the coolest end of the greenhouse where they are placed on shelves as close to the glass as possible without the leaves actually touching it, to give maximum light. Light is essential to ensure complete ripening of the pseudobulbs, as would occur in the wild. At the same time, watering is gradually reduced, and in some plants dispensed with altogether. While in this inactive state,

Masdevallia yungasensis. Masdevallias grow continuously throughout the year and, therefore, need constant watering.

therefore do not need to be free-flowering. In cultivation they may need to be given additional encouragement in order to produce flowers. This is particularly true of standard cymbidiums which can become lazy. If you have one or two plants in your collection that have not bloomed for a number of years, despite being large and apparently healthy and capable of flowering, try giving them a more severe winter's rest. Do this by allowing the temperature to lower to the minimum, and keeping the plants drier for a longer period. Do not worry if they begin to shrivel; they will plump up again quite quickly when you resume watering in the early spring, by which time your plant may well be showing its flower spike.

With approach of spring, the new growths will appear. This is a sign that the plant is waking up and once again starting to grow. This is the best time to repot those orchids that need it, provided they are not flowering, and return them to their summer quarters. New growth is followed by the development of new roots, and as soon as the new roots can be seen around the base of the pseudobulb, normal watering can resume. Before that, water lightly and spray the foliage to maintain some moisture. Take care not to allow water to get into the funnel of new growths, where it may cause rot, particularly if it remains there overnight. Once the new roots are taking up moisture from the pot, any shrivelled pseudobulbs will soon plump up, and they should remain like this all summer.

FEEDING

There are many proprietary brands of fertilizer that are ideal for greenhouse plants and which can be used for orchids, usually at half strength. Specialist orchid nurseries and the better garden centres stock feed made specifically for orchids, which is obviously the best choice.

Some orchids can take more feed than others: the faster-growing lycastes and their allies, thunias and calanthes, all produce their season's pseudobulbs in about four months, and can be fed at every watering over their growing period. The majority of orchids, including cymbidiums, odontoglossums and dendrobiums, can be fed during the summer at every other watering. Start to apply feed, mixed with water, at every third watering from early spring. Gradually increase this until the plants are getting a regular feed

the natural process of shrivelling will take place in some species. This slight buckling of pseudobulbs is normal and often helps the plants to flower better. It is not to be confused with the dangerous dehydration associated with incorrect watering, mentioned above.

The monopodial orchids, which include the vandas and their allies, as well as phalaenopsis, will also slow or cease their growth, and this can be seen by the white, papery covering, the velamen, enclosing the root tips, which cease to be green and active.

Some orchids reproduce themselves quite adequately by vegetative means – dividing and subdividing – and every other watering throughout the summer. As the pseudobulbs begin to mature, gradually lessen this in preparation for the coming winter. Start by using a nitrate-based feed in the spring to encourage plenty of good healthy growth, and as this matures, change to a phosphate-based feed to encourage flowering. Once you have settled on a particular type of feed, do not change to another brand halfway through the growing cycle. If you feel that your plants would do better with another type of feed, make the change-over at the start of the growing season and continue with that for the year.

Always read the label, and use fertilizers according to the manufacturer's instructions. If in doubt give less feed rather than more. Only feed orchids which are growing well and which are healthy. Do not give food to sickly plants or those that have lost their roots. They have no means of taking up the fertilizer from the pot, the chemicals will build up in the compost causing an inbalance of salts, and when new roots eventually appear, they may easily be burnt by these concentrated chemicals. This can also happen where plants are overfed. Avoid any build-up of unwanted fertilizer by using clean water at every third application, to ensure that any residue is washed through the compost.

Once you stop feeding your orchids in the autumn, discard any left-over liquid fertilizer or use it on some other crop, but do not keep it for the following spring for your orchids. The chemical make-up may have changed slightly and what was previously a good feed for your orchids, may turn into something quite hazardous.

Any orchids that are showing a slight yellowing of their foliage may have been given too much light, or it may be that they should have been repotted and are lacking nutrients. You can spray these plants with a foliar feed once or twice a week to improve the colour of their leaves.

(See pp.53–55 for orchid ailments that may arise due to cultivation problems.)

POTTING

The majority of orchids in cultivation are epiphytes, or hybrids that are descended from epiphytic species. When grown in pots, these need an open, well-drained, soil-free compost. One of the most successful composts, and one that is easy to obtain and use, is made of chunks of fir bark, obtained from pine-forest trees, which is a sustainable resource. The bark is slow to decompose, and as it does so, it releases nutrients into the pot and these are absorbed by the roots. To these basic bark chippings you can add dried sphagnum moss, horticultural foam, or any other aggregate such as Perlite or Perlag. This will keep the compost open and prevent it from clogging as the bark deteriorates. Mixing in sphagnum or horticultural foam produces a compost that will stay wetter for longer periods, which is useful if you cannot get to water your orchids as often as you would like.

An alternative to this organic compost is the man-made horticultural produce called Rockwool, which has the appearance of grey cottonwool. This unlikely, but very successful, medium for orchids is made from spun volcanic rock. Stonewool is similar. Many of the orchids purchased from garden centres and large stores, especially around holiday time, are potted in this inorganic compound because it is widely used in The Netherlands, where many of these orchids are bred and raised. Its advantages are that it does not decompose and because of this you can keep the plants wetter for much of the time without the danger of rot setting in. Again, this is useful where you cannot water your orchids so often.

Two types of Rockwool are available from suppliers of orchid sundries: absorbent and non-absorbent. Some growers prefer to mix the two brands together, which ensures that the compost never becomes too saturated and that there are always drier areas within the pot for the roots to breathe. Whichever compost is used, this is an important point to remember. In their natural state, most of the orchid's roots would be exposed to the air.

When potting with a bark mix, the plant is firmed down using your fingers to push it down into the pot. Rockwool and Stonewool is simply poured into the pot and left fairly loose, without any pushing down. It must not be compressed or the roots will be unable to penetrate it. When first potted, you may need to stake a plant to hold it firm.

Do not combine the organic compost with the inorganic, and if you are swapping a plant from one mix to the other, be sure to remove all traces of the old compost first. The two composts are not compatible, nor will your orchids grow well in a mixture of bark and

PLATE II

Cymbidium species
and hybrids

C. Pontac

C. Gorey

C. Madame Giscard

All flowers are shown at
approximately half size

C. devonianum

C. Les Landes

C. Cotil Point

C. Goldrun

C. lowianum var. concolor

Rockwool. Also, to add bark to Rockwool defeats the object of having a cleaner, more durable medium for your orchids to grow in.

Apart from the differences in the watering between the mixes, there is the matter of artificial feeding. In the organic compounds, the orchids will derive benefit from the slowly decomposing material, from which they can gain useful nutrients. This means that any artificial fertilizer given is supplementary to what they are already getting from the compost; therefore, the feeding regime can be light. Plants growing in Rockwool on the other hand, will gain nothing from their rooting material and are completely reliant upon the application of feed given with the water. The addition of fertilizer, therefore, becomes more necessary and must be looked at more carefully. A regular and balanced programme of feeding is important for the welfare of the orchids (see pp.28–29).

Excellent results can be achieved with either medium but when moving a plant from one type of compost to the other, it may take that plant some time to adjust to the new conditions. If you wish to try both types of compost, keep the orchids separated and observe their progress over a period of at least two years before deciding which is the best method for you.

REPOTTING

The spring is the best time to undertake any repotting, when the new growths are getting under way, and the new roots soon to be made can penetrate immediately into the fresh compost. Where a plant is flowering at this time of the year, repot it as soon as possible after the flowers have finished.

An orchid is in need of repotting when the leading pseudobulb or growth has reached the rim of the pot and there is no room for future development. Or when a plant has become root-bound, and as often happens with cymbidiums, when a plant has lifted itself above the rim of the pot. On average, orchids need repotting every other year, the exception being the deciduous ones, such as pleiones, calanthes and thunias, which require annual repotting. Deciduous orchids like a richer compost, which can be based on peat substitute with sand or Perlite mixed in.

Dendrobium miyakei is a pretty, free-flowering species. Dendrobiums require a decided winter rest to flower well.

Encyclia cochleata produces spikes of up to 10 flowers. It blooms freely in a cool or intermediate house.

Before you start any potting, decide on the best area to work, and have ready sheets of newspaper to lay out and work on, a pair of secateurs, a sharp knife and a bucket for waste material, such as the old roots and compost. It is also a good ideal to have handy a jar of methylated spirits, into which you can dip the tools before and after use to sterilize them. Have a supply of suitably-sized pots – plastic ones are fine for most orchids – and a few pieces of polystyrene chips of the sort used as packing material. They are usually available from the same source as your orchid compost.

An orchid can be completely repotted by cleaning out all old roots and compost, or merely 'dropped on', as is usual with young plants. In 'dropping on' a plant, you do not disturb the root ball at all, but after knocking the plant out of its pot, simply place it into another, larger container and fill in around with compost.

Dropping on

To drop on a young plant that has filled its pot, but has no surplus back bulbs or extensive growth that needs reducing, remove it from its pot with a few sharp taps on the edge of the workbench. This should reveal a healthy ball of solid, white roots. Remove the old crocking from in between the roots without disturbing the root ball. Take a slightly larger pot and place a layer of crocks in the base. Cover this with a thin layer of compost and place the plant in the new pot. The base of the plant should be slightly below the rim of the pot. If the plant is standing too high, remove a little of the compost from the bottom of the pot; if it is too low, add more compost to the bottom until the plant is in the right position. Holding the plant upright, fill in with compost all round. If you are using bark, this can be firmed down with your fingers and thumbs; Rockwool should be poured in and then the pot and plant given a few taps on the bench to settle it in place. When using Rockwool, be sure to use disposable gloves and a mask to protect against the minute fibres, which can be inhaled or penetrate the skin to cause irritation. Finish with the compost just below the rim of the pot for ease of watering. Allow the plant to settle in its new pot for a couple of days before giving a good watering, which can then be resumed as normal.

Total repotting

Total repotting takes more time and care. If you have not attempted to repot an orchid before, it is a good idea to use the drop-on method until you feel familiar with it before attempting total repotting.

Orchids that have been in their existing pot for some time may be quite difficult to dislodge. The roots will have adhered to the sides of the pot and you may have to run a long-bladed knife around the inside to loosen them. Once out of its pot, remove all the old compost so the plant becomes bare-rooted. At this stage you can check the roots and remove all the dead ones – orchid roots are not permanent, and it is quite natural for the old roots to die as the leaves above are shed; you are then left with a leafless back bulb. Where there is a surplus of back bulbs, these need to be removed from the plant, which should always have more pseudobulbs in leaf than out of leaf. Cut off the old back bulbs by using a sharp knife, slicing between the pseudobulbs to sever the rhizome that joins them. Place these on one side (if you want to, you can propagate from them to produce further plants).

Take the main plant and cut away all dead roots. These will be blackened and the outer covering will peel away leaving the wiry core. The live roots will be supporting the younger pseudobulbs, and can be trimmed back to about 15cm (6in), if they are very long. It is better to cut them back at this stage, than to have over-long roots break or crack, which may well set up a rot in the new pot. You may find that having reduced the size of your plant, it will go back into the same sized pot.

Where you have a large plant that has new growths showing on various sides, it may be possible to split the plant in two or more, provided you can leave at least three pseudobulbs with leaves on each piece. Sever the plant between the old pseudobulbs and pull apart. Trim each division and put each separately into a pot big enough for a further two years' growth. Do not be tempted to use a pot larger than this: overpotting will lead to overwatering; an orchid that has too great a volume of compost around the roots will be unable to

absorb the moisture fast enough, and if there is still a surplus around the roots, they will die.

If you have divided a plant, remember to write a new label for each piece. It is surprising how quickly you can forget which was which where you have more than a few plants.

CORK BARK RAFTS

In a small greenhouse there is the constant problem of finding sufficient space to accommodate the ever-increasing orchid collection. Where a variety of plants is grown, you can attach suitable species to cork bark rafts and suspend them from the roof or the greenhouse sides. This saves valuable staging space and often benefits the plants, which grow all the better. Also, it is fun to watch aerial roots form and extend into the moisture-laden atmosphere.

The species most suitable for bark culture are those that produce long, creeping rhizomes, or have an upward habit of growth that is difficult to contain in a flower pot. Some examples are *Oncidium flexuosum*, *Epigeneium amplum*, and several of the bulbophyllums,

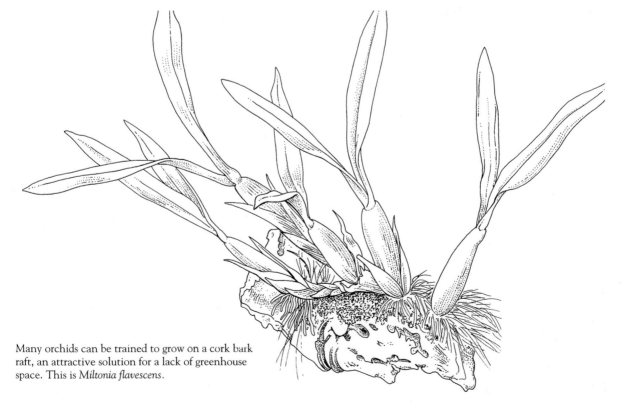

Many orchids can be trained to grow on a cork bark raft, an attractive solution for a lack of greenhouse space. This is *Miltonia flavescens*.

but there are many others that are just as suitable. A number of *Dendrobium* species produce long, drooping canes. In pots these have to be tied upright, but on bark the plants are transformed: their long, thin canes are far more attractive and comfortable when allowed to droop. These orchids will also benefit from the extra light they receive when hanging closer to the glass in the greenhouse roof. However, in this position, they will dry out much faster, and will need constant spraying to keep them moist.

While cork bark is the ideal material, you can use other barks if they are to hand, but avoid resinous pines. A good rough surface will help the plant to get its roots into the crevices where they will establish themselves more quickly. You can try using half a coconut shell, or make your own wooden rafts or baskets. Another nice idea, where there is sufficient room

Oncidium Star Wars has bright yellow, large-lipped flowers and is one of a range of brightly coloured *Oncidium* hybrids.

at one end of the greenhouse, is to obtain a branch or stout bough from an oak or apple tree and fix this into position. To this you can attach a number of little species. They will establish themselves in a short time, and can be left in position for several years. If you do not have room for such an orchid tree, fix a piece of trellis against one wall, and attach your hanging species on their bark rafts to this.

How it's done

Select a plant and use a piece of bark that is the right size and length to take it comfortably. Bore a small hole at one end of the bark and thread a piece of wire through the hole so that you can hang it up. Take the plant out of its pot and remove the old compost. Trim any dead roots.

You will need padding to place between the plant and the bark. The best material for this is coconut fibre, as supplied by orchid sundries firms or specialist nurseries. Place a wad of fibre on top of the bark and posi-

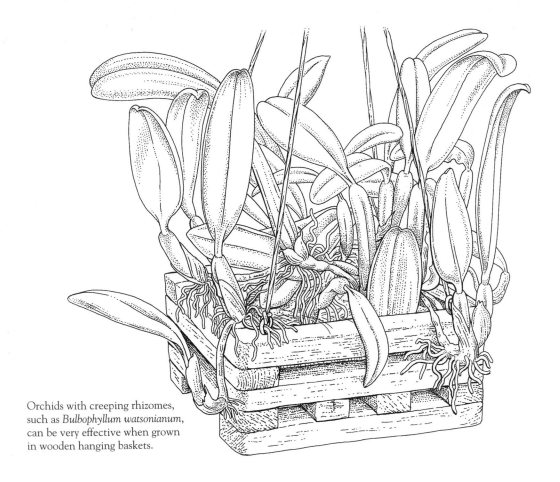

Orchids with creeping rhizomes, such as *Bulbophyllum watsonianum*, can be very effective when grown in wooden hanging baskets.

tion the plant above this. Allow for the way the plant is to grow forward, and leave plenty of room for its upward or downward habit – the oldest pseudobulbs should be placed at the bottom of the support if it is growing upwards. Use plastic-coated wire, of the type sold in garden centres, to tie your plant into position. Take the wire around the plant and its support, slotting it between the pseudobulbs and taking care not to cut into the green parts of the orchid. Two or three ties should be sufficient, but be sure to pull the wire tight, and twist it off using a pair of pliers. When you have finished, the plant should be secure on the bark. If it is wobbly and can be moved about, you will need to tighten the wire.

The plant can remain on its mount for several years, and it will only be necessary from time to time to place extra pads of the fibre underneath the extending growths. In time the plant will have produced roots which will adhere to the bark, and you can then remove the wire supports and the plant will remain firmly in place. Immediately after placing the plant on its piece of bark, give it a good spraying with water and keep it moist from then on. If you consider it is becoming too dry at any time, place it in a bucket of water for up to half an hour. You can do this as often as necessary to keep the plant moist enough to prevent any shrivelling of its pseudobulbs.

Wooden hanging baskets

Many orchids look good when grown in hanging wooden baskets, especially those species that have drooping or pendent flower spikes. Plastic aquatic plant pots also make ideal hanging containers for orchids. To place a plant in one of these use the same method of potting as dropping on, making sure that the plant is firm in the basket. It may be necessary to cut off the bottom of the root ball, if the basket is shallower than the pot from which the plant came.

PLATE III

Dendrobium species and hybrids

D. Thwaitesii

D. Aporon

D. Pink Beauty

D. Stardust

D. infundibulum

D. nobile var. *albiflorum*

All flowers are shown at approximately half size

PROPAGATION

ORCHIDS WITH PSEUDOBULBS

Most orchids with pseudobulbs can be propagated at repotting time simply by removing any surplus back bulbs. Back bulbs are the oldest pseudobulbs; they have shed their leaves and their roots have died. While they remain on the plant, they support the younger growths. However, if their number becomes greater than the pseudobulbs in leaf, the plant is not balanced, and they will become a drain on it. Ideally, a plant should consist of three or four pseudobulbs in leaf, with perhaps one or two out of leaf. Once a plant has more pseudobulbs out of leaf than in leaf, most if not all the leafless pseudobulbs should be removed. This is a rough guide, however, and all plants vary. The deciduous lycastes, for example, will carry leaves only on the leading, or previous season's, pseudobulbs, so with these and allied plants, there will always be a cluster of leafless pseudobulbs.

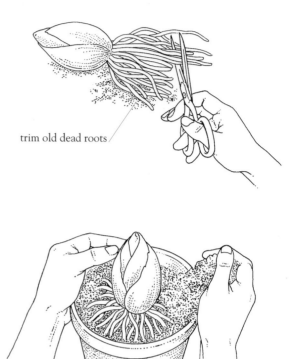

trim old dead roots

To propagate an orchid with pseudobulbs, first remove one or more back bulbs using a sharp knife (left). Remove the old roots (top), and then pot up the individual bulbs.

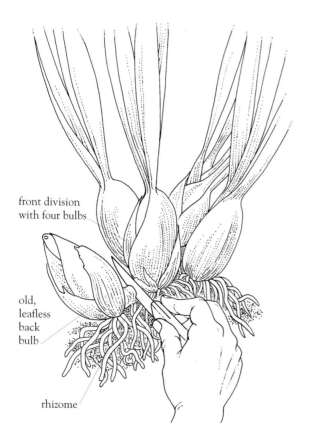

front division with four bulbs

old, leafless back bulb

rhizome

It is often necessary to cut off back bulbs to prevent the plant from becoming too large for the accommodation available. The surplus back bulbs are removed and, on cymbidiums, the old leaf bases or bracts are stripped away. The roots are then removed, leaving just enough to anchor the back bulbs when they are repotted. Split them into individual bulbs, otherwise it is unlikely that they will grow. Choose only those that are hard and firm. Any that are shrivelled, or brown and soft, will be dead; healthy ones have dormant growths, or eyes, around their base. These can be seen as a small, green or brown triangle.

Place the individual back bulbs in a community pot with compost. Take care not to bury them too deeply as this could rot off the new growth, which will appear from the base within a few weeks. Once the new growth has started, new roots will soon follow. At this stage they can be potted separately and grown on for a few years until they reach flowering size. An alternative is to place the back bulbs in a plastic bag with a little damp moss to encourage early growth. Inspect the bag regularly and as you see back bulbs sprouting new growth, take them out and pot them up.

ORCHIDS WITHOUT PSEUDOBULBS
Orchids that do not produce pseudobulbs, including monopodials, are less easy to propagate. Paphiopedilums are best grown on into large plants until they can be divided. Phalaenopsis seldom propagate readily, but will produce new growth from their base if the centre of the plant becomes damaged or rots. Occasionally, new growths will appear on old flower spikes and, when they develop their own roots, these young plants can be removed and potted up on their own. This may take between six and 12 months.

Other monopodial orchids, including the vandas, are harder to propagate. Sometimes, they will naturally produce new growths from their base, and when large enough, these can be removed and potted up. However, to encourage these new growths artificially is a slow and unreliable practice. A method used with long-caned orchids, such as dendrobiums, is to remove an older, leafless cane and cut it into pieces, which are then laid in a seed tray or placed upright around a community pot and left to produce new growths.

Propagation tips
There are a few points to remember when embarking on a programme of propagation. Be sure that propagations are really wanted beforehand. You can increase the number of plants you have, but you will only be producing more of the same, and it will be several years before you see any flowers. Nevertheless, it is fun to grow a new plant from an old back bulb, and these propagations can be swapped for others from fellow growers who have varieties different from your own.

Only propagate from healthy stock. If you suspect a plant of having virus disease because of streaking through the leaves, do not produce more of the same. The virus will be present in all parts of the plant, and it can be easily spread by accident or by pests to other plants nearby.

If you have a tray of back bulbs waiting to grow, it is of little advantage to keep them for longer than six months. If they have not started to grow in that time, they are unlikely to grow at all, and are best discarded. It may be that they were too old, or had no spare embryo growths, or these may have become damaged.

However, as much as you may want to propagate from your favourite plants, do not risk the health of a strong plant by reducing it too much. Every time you divide a plant, or remove old pseudobulbs, there is some stress caused, and a slight risk of rot setting in on the cut part of the rhizome, and a plant could be lost.

4

ORCHIDS IN THE HOME

It is perfectly possible to grow some orchids indoors. Indeed, orchid hybrids are now produced in their tens of thousands especially for the houseplant trade. These are available in the more popular genera, such as phalaenopsis, which adapt most easily to growing indoors where the light is generally poorer, and the temperature more constant, with less variation between day and night. The range of phalaenopsis available has multiplied greatly with the introduction of modern hybrids, which have extended the colours to encompass all shades from white, through yellow, pink and mauve-red. Phalaenopsis has now become the top indoor orchid, thriving in the shadier conditions and warmth of the average dwelling. Requiring similar conditions, the mottled-leaved paphiopedilums are also extremely good for home growing. Other popular orchids include cymbidiums – a large variety of the smaller types can be grown in cooler, well-lit areas – and the miltoniopsis, which will thrive in the same atmosphere. These, along with a few other easily grown orchids, can do extremely well indoors with the minimum of care.

The main difference between greenhouse and indoor culture is that in the home, the orchids adapt to the conditions there, and do not have a specific environment created for them. Less time is spent getting the atmosphere right, and there is not the same day-to-day regime. In some ways growing orchids indoors can be easier and less demanding. If you are away from home all day, for example, the orchids are unlikely to have suffered upon your return from overheating, which can

so easily occur in a greenhouse should the ventilators be left closed on a hot day. Another advantage of growing orchids indoors is that you are with them much more of the time. This means that you can attend to their needs more quickly. A plant in need of moisture will be watered immediately, and not left until you have the time to spend in the greenhouse. Likewise, you will notice as soon as a plant is standing in direct sun, and move it to a more suitable position before any harm is done.

Growing orchids indoors is also much less expensive as there is no additional outlay on a greenhouse and equipment. You need only a few humidity trays and at least two maximum/minimum thermometers to start you off.

POSITION

Within the home there are many areas where orchids will grow. A light windowsill facing south can provide an ideal position during the winter when the low sun can benefit the plants without the danger of burning the leaves. In summer a north- or east-facing window will be better. If you cannot move your plants to a shadier position, grow them behind a slatted blind or net curtains so that they receive good light but not direct sun. This is the same whether you are growing orchids indoors or in the greenhouse. The shade-loving phalaenopsis and paphiopedilums will grow away from a window and be at home in the centre of a room where light is coming in from one or more sides.

Places to avoid growing orchids are any dark corners where little light reaches, or close to a source of heat such as a radiator. Beware also of your plants standing in a cold draught.

Phalaenopsis, here P. Brother Lancer, are among the most popular orchids for growing in the home.

MOISTURE

One of the biggest problems for orchids indoors is dehydration, either through a dry atmosphere or dry potting compost. Plants that are dehydrated will show this by limp foliage, or by leaves becoming whitish from the tips, the effect eventually running down to the base. To avoid problems caused by lack of moisture, grow your orchids on a humidity tray filled with pebbles and containing some water. In this way the plants can benefit from a little moisture evaporating from the water in the tray. But be sure not to let the plants actually stand in water. This may lead to the compost becoming too wet for too long a period, which will cause the loss of roots and other associated overwatering problems (see pp.53–55).

During the summer months, light overhead spraying with a small, hand-held spray bottle full of water will assist in keeping the foliage fresh and free from dust.

OTHER CULTIVATION DETAILS

The same details of culture apply wherever you grow your orchids, and as far as possible, the same temperature range should be adhered to (see pp.18–19). Be sure to place a thermometer near them, so that you can monitor the night-time temperature. You may need to move your orchids around to find the best position for them where conditions are as near as possible to those they would receive in a greenhouse.

Those orchids that can take up a lot of room, and that like good light to flower well, such as cymbidiums, can be placed outdoors for the summer, in the same way as greenhouse plants are taken out to be given a cooler, fresher environment while they are in active growth.

While the range of orchids you can grow well indoors is limited, this is often a good way to start a collection, choosing a few of the easier varieties to see how you get along. Some growers use both methods, having some orchids as houseplants, and others requiring more specific treatment in a greenhouse. Whichever way you decide to grow your orchids, they will bring much joy and fun into your life. You can fuss over them for long hours, noting their every sign of growth, the speed with which their flower spikes develop, and, finally, enjoy their delightful and long-lasting blooms.

Miltoniopsis, here M. St Helier 'Lavender Charm', can be grown indoors with the minimum of fuss.

5

PESTS AND DISEASES

Orchids are an undesirable host for most pests that attack other greenhouse plants. Although the number of pests from which they suffer is, therefore, small, these can cause a considerable amount of damage if allowed to remain unchecked. Controlling them should be a routine job on the principle that prevention is better than cure.

There are numerous insecticides to choose from. Bear in mind that where one type of pesticide is used regularly, some pests can build up an immunity, so it is as well to change the chemicals you use from time to time. Always take care to follow the manufacturer's instructions, and take all the necessary precautions when handling poisonous substances. There are alternatives to chemicals: you may prefer to use methylated spirits, which can be used as a contact killer for most pests. Before spraying your plants, remove any blooms which would be spoilt.

There are two ways in which pests and diseases can enter a greenhouse. Firstly, there are the indigenous pests that can be brought into the collection on new plants, and secondly, there are the pests that will live outside in the summer and enter the greenhouse of their own accord. Watch out for the latter mainly in the spring and autumn, when they are attracted and encouraged to breed by the warmth of the greenhouse. Cleanliness in the greenhouse goes a long way to preventing the appearance of moulds and bacteria. Pick up any fallen leaves and dead flowers so that you have no decaying matter left under the staging where it will encourage problems.

Coelogyne massangeana is a robust plant with long, pendent flower spikes bearing abundant small blooms.

MAJOR PESTS
Red spider mite
This mite is pale orange-yellow and only just discernible with the naked eye: a hand-lens is necessary for real study. Look for red spider mite on the undersides of the leaves, particularly on cymbidiums, where it will breed in great numbers in a very short period. The young are hatched from eggs.

In large colonies this mite will protect itself with a very fine web, which is most easily seen on the stems of the flower buds, but the mite affects leaves and buds alike. When it attacks small, developing buds, it damages the surface of the sepals, causing deformities when the flowers open. In bad cases, the buds turn yellow and drop off.

Red spider mite will also attack the softer-leaved dendrobiums and odontoglossums. Look for silvery-white patches on the undersides of leaves. This is where the mite has sucked the sap and killed the leaf cells. In a short time a secondary infection will attack the damaged areas, turning them black.

One good way to discourage this pest on leaves is to spray them on the undersides frequently during the summer, and at any other time whenever possible, as it prefers a hot, dry atmosphere. The best method of control is insecticide spray. You can repeat this once monthly, or where a bad attack has been discovered, every 7–10 days, to eradicate the new generation hatching from the eggs.

Scale insects
There are many different types of scale insects. Once adult, these settle down in one place and cover themselves in a scaly membrane, which is usually whitish,

and in one type is accompanied by a woolly substance, but it is not to be confused with mealy bug (see below).

Scale is found mostly on cattleyas and cymbidiums, as well as a number of other orchids. On cymbidiums, it is usually the harder type that is seen most on leaves and pseudobulbs. When removed, it leaves a small, yellow patch, where it has damaged the leaf. On cattleyas, a softer type is more often seen and this can build up into large colonies, coating the pseudobulbs and rhizomes underneath the sheaths, and destroying dormant growth buds and new root tips. Eventually, it can lead to the destruction of the plant.

New additions coming into the collection should always be checked for scale by peeling back the covering sheaths. This pest is persistent and vigorous and the

best form of control is to use an insecticidal soap solution in a bucket of water. Dip each plant up to the rim of the pot (upside down) and, using a small stiff paintbrush, dislodge the scale by careful brushing. You can also brush with methylated spirits to dislodge and kill the scale. For long-term control use a systemic insecticide. Keep all affected plants together and watch out for the scale's return. It may return several times before finally being stamped out.

Mealy bug

This small insect is another sap-sucking pest. It lives under a white, mealy powder and is more manoeuvrable than scale. Like scale, it is usually introduced on plants coming into the greenhouse. Mealy bug, which can greatly weaken a plant if left unchecked, is found mainly in the axils of the leaves of most orchids. Control is the same as for scale.

Wilsonara Widecombe Fair has tall, branching flower spikes, producing a Christmas tree-like effect.

Slugs and snails

These are too well known to need any description, but are, nonetheless, quite dangerous pests. The warm, moist conditions in the orchid house are well suited to slugs and snails, and they need to be continually controlled. They will attack young growths and root tips, and a large garden snail will make a sizable hole in a pseudobulb overnight. Mostly they eat the softer flower spikes and buds, and can also eat their way right through a flower spike overnight.

Some growers like to have a resident toad or two in the greenhouse, in which case slug pellets must not be used. If you do not want to poison the slugs and snails, try putting a small wad of cotton wool around the base of the flower spikes to protect them. If you find a pseudobulb has been badly damaged, treat the hole as soon as you discover it and before any decay can set in. Clean out the wound to remove any secretion using a horticultural wipe to dry it up. Dust the hole with horticultural sulphur or charcoal. Keep the plant dry for a few days until the wound has had a chance to heal.

A small, brownish snail, known as the garlic snail, can become a nuisance among young seedlings. An easy control is to place thin slices of apple or potato on the surface of the compost overnight. The next morning the snails can be found congregating on the underside. Replace with fresh apple or potato until you find no more snails.

An extremely old hybrid, *Zygopetalum* Perrenoudii is still in cultivation today.

Greenfly

Greenfly will get into the greenhouse from outside and will attack buds and new growths and breed rapidly. They can be wiped from buds with no apparent damage, but when the flower opens their effects can be seen. On cymbidiums it will show up as small bumps.

Control greenfly with an aerosol spray, or wash the pest off by rinsing the buds in water, to which has been added a wetting agent.

Ants

These are comparatively harmless in the greenhouse, but they will encourage and spread greenfly. They also do damage if they set up a nest in a pot as they will quickly break down the compost, clogging it up. If you find an infested plant, soak it in a bucket of water until all the ants are dead, and then repot it as soon as possible.

Thrips

Like red spider mite, these pests are too small to be seen easily: it is usually the damage they have caused that is seen first as they are sap-suckers. Look for semi-transparent pin-holes on the foliage of most orchids, especially on the new growths and on flowers. Use a systemic insecticide to control thrips.

Springtails

These are small, grey, wingless, but fast-moving insects. They can be found on the staging, in upturned pots or among the crocks and compost. In small quantities springtails are insufficient to do any real harm. However, among seedlings they can cause damage by breaking down the compost and even damaging root tips of young plants. Springtails breed in the compost, so water your plants with an insecticide solution, allowing it to go over the staging and floor as well.

PLATE IV

A selection of orchid species

Encylia linkiana

*Mexicoa
ghiesbrectiana*

Dendrochilum latifolium

Oerstedella centradenia

*All flowers are shown at
approximately half size*

Maxillaria coccinea

Brassia verrucosa

Zygopetalum crinitum

Maxillaria aracnita

Moss flies

These small, blackish flies can be seen flying around just above the surface of the compost. While the flies do no harm themselves, the larvae, hatched from eggs laid in the compost, will feed on the softer pieces within the compost, breaking it down in a similar way to springtails. The larvae will also attack small seedlings and they will eat into the base of the plants, destroying the root system. They are extremely small, whitish and maggot-like and can be found close to the surface of the compost when this is turned over gently by hand.

Control is not easy, since the flies breed and increase at an alarming rate in high temperatures. The adults can be killed off with aerosols, but within a day or two a second generation will have emerged to lay further eggs, and so on. Spraying in rapid succession is, therefore, necessary to break their life-cycle. Like the springtails, the larvae can be killed by adding insecticide when watering, after which the dead larvae will come to the surface.

OTHER PESTS

There are a number of other pests that may occasionally crop up in an orchid house, such as woodlice, encouraged by rotting leaves and any other waste material left under the staging and elsewhere. Vine weevils will eat parts of flowers and soft leaves. Being nocturnal, they are seldom seen during the day. Search for them with a torch after dark while you are looking for slugs.

Mice

Mice are attracted into the greenhouse by the warmth, mostly during the autumn and winter, and will make their home in any empty flower pots or boxes stored near heating systems. They will eat pollen from flowers, bite into buds, root tips, seedlings and even gnaw pseudobulbs, doing an amazing amount of damage in one night. Although not very frequently met with in the greenhouse, the problems that they can cause should not be underestimated, but they are easily controlled by setting humane traps and setting them free well away from the greenhouse.

Calanthe Gorey is one of a new breed of *Calanthe* hybrids showing enriched colour.

Bees

In the early spring when there is a show of orchids in bloom, spells of bright weather will bring out the first bees, at a time when few, if any, flowers are to be found in the garden outside. The bees are quickly attracted to the orchids, where in a few minutes they will have pollinated any number of flowers. Once pollinated, instead of lasting many weeks, the flowers will turn red and within a couple of days collapse as fertilization takes place. It is usually the large and beautiful bumble bee which fits perfectly into a cymbidium flower that does more harm than the smaller honey bee. The only way to ensure that bees are kept out of the greenhouse is to cover the ventilator openings with a fine mesh or net curtains, and make sure there are no other small openings.

DISEASES AND AILMENTS
Black marks

Orchids, especially cymbidiums, are rather prone to getting black tips or odd black marks on their foliage. These can be caused by such cultural problems as overwatering, cold draughts, or a combination of the two. During the summer ugly black patches can be the result of sun scorch.

Provided that the black marking remains on the older foliage and is not excessive, there is usually little to worry about. For neatness, the black tips can be trimmed back carefully with a pair of scissors. During the autumn, most orchids will naturally discard some, if not all, of their foliage. Therefore, at this time of the year, yellow leaves on the oldest pseudobulbs are to be expected.

Excessive leaf-loss

Yellow leaves that appear on the older pseudobulbs during the autumn or immediately after repotting are quite natural and not always a cause for concern. However, should excessive premature foliage-loss happen at any time, there may be some other cause. Knock the plant out of its pot and examine the roots. From their condition you can tell whether it has been over-watered, or the roots attacked by some pest. Otherwise, the compost may be in a poor state, and this will cause the roots to die. Repot as soon as you can, reducing the number of pseudobulbs and cutting back the dead roots.

The striking flowers of *Gongora maculata*. Fanciful blooms resembling winged insects in flight are typical of the genus.

Yellow foliage

Orchids whose foliage has turned from a good healthy green to a sickly yellow may be suffering from a lack of nutrition. This is especially likely with small, fast-growing seedlings in small pots. Repotting into fresh compost will bring the colour back into the leaves, and a light foliar feed sprayed onto the foliage will also help.

Viruses

Prolonged exposure to cold, combined with high humidity, gross overfeeding or overwatering and general bad culture can weaken a plant and expose it to a virus infection. Several viruses affect orchids. In cymbidiums, the cymbidium mosaic virus appears as a white flecking in the new growth, intermittent along the length of the leaf, in bad cases forming a diamond pattern. As the foliage ages, these markings turn black, as a secondary infection attacks the leaf. This can cause premature yellowing of the remainder of the leaf. In other orchids, viruses will take on a similar appearance or pitting of the leaf surface. In very bad cases, it can kill a plant. If you suspect virus in a plant, isolate it to prevent it being spread to other plants.

There is no cure for viruses, but where a plant is mildly affected, good culture and a slightly higher temperature will assist in retarding its progress. Viruses can be spread by practically all the pests previously described, as well as by knives used for cutting leaves or flower spikes, or roots at repotting time. Therefore, it is best to sterilize all cutting instruments by passing them through a flame or immersing them in a solution of methylated spirits.

Blemishes

A number of blemishes may appear on the foliage of orchids in the form of black spots, markings or rings, and soft pseudobulbs on mature plants. These are caused by cultural faults rather than a disease or virus. Miltoniopsis, for example, are particularly prone to black spots on their foliage owing to their delicate nature. Allow more ventilation and a slightly drier atmosphere to prevent the spots from spreading, although those already present will not disappear. These troubles usually reach their peak during the autumn and winter, when a correct balance between the temperature and humidity is harder to maintain.

Decreasing pseudobulbs

In a healthy specimen that has pseudobulbs, these should increase in size each year until their maximum is reached. If you can see that the new pseudobulbs are getting smaller than the previous ones each year, take a look at your cultural techniques. Try moving the plant to a warmer or cooler position in the greenhouse and check to see that you are giving it the right conditions.

Soft pseudobulbs

Ageing pseudobulbs will occasionally turn brown and become soft, sometimes while they are still supporting leaves. This may be caused by a rot that has developed in the plant. Cut off the diseased pseudobulb and dust the severed area with powdered horticultural sulphur or charcoal. A close look at the pseudobulb you have removed may reveal a slug hole at the base – the cause of the problem.

Transparent new growth

New growths that, for no apparent reason, become transparent, later turning brown, may have water lodged inside the funnel of leaves. These new growths need to be removed to prevent the rot spreading, and again the cut portion treated to dry it up. Plants that have been treated in this way will need to be placed on a shelf where you can keep them on the dry side until any wound has healed and completely dried up. Within a short time they will produce further new growth.

Aborting buds

One of the most disappointing aspects of orchid growing is when developing buds, promising flowering to come, instead turn yellow and drop off, which usually occurs at a point when the buds are almost fully developed and about to open. The buds abort in this way when conditions are not suitable. In the greenhouse it may be cool, sunless days, which you cannot do much about, or overwatering. If a plant is about to flower, try not to change the conditions until after the flowers have opened. Bringing it indoors to enjoy the blooms before they are open can be enough for them to abort.

Miltoniopsis Venus × Pulchra is an older *Miltoniopsis* hybrid that lacks the perfect flower shape.

Leave it in the greenhouse until the flowers are fully open, and then bring the plant indoors, where it can remain for the duration of the flowering, if you wish.

6

EXHIBITING ORCHIDS

There are many good reasons to join one of the many amateur orchid societies. Apart from having knowledgeable growers with whom to share your interest, there are regular meetings and lectures to attend; there are also table shows and annual exhibitions, and sooner or later you will be persuaded to enter your own orchids in the classes.

The way in which a plant is presented for display can tip the scales when it comes to a 'photo finish' between two plants. Any orchid can be suitable for exhibition, and does not have to be a very expensive variety. Often, the less expensive but showy species will be placed above a rather less attractive hybrid. Do not feel that your plants are not good enough – you will probably be surprised and delighted at your first result! All plants must, however, be healthy, well grown and free from any pests or disease. It can be embarrassing if someone finds a lone greenfly, or worse, on one of your plants, and you would not wish to spread any pests onto nearby plants belonging to someone else. Usually, the show secretary will check all entries before the show opens, and quietly point out any missed pest.

TRAINING FLOWERS

Preparing a plant for the show bench can start when the young buds have first left the sheath or as they begin to separate. At this stage they will require training in the right direction – away from the foliage as much as possible, to show off the blooms to their best advantage. With cymbidiums, odontoglossums and those with long sprays of flowers, try not to interfere

Odontoglossum Monte Ube × O. Panise is a superb yellow variety with some spotting.

with the natural carriage of the flower spike. Wherever possible, the length that carries the buds should be allowed to arch naturally. The base of the flower spike can be supported with a thin bamboo cane, inserted into the compost, close to the spike but away from the side of the pot, which is where most of the roots are. With more erect flower spikes, cut the cane just below the topmost flowers; with the arching varieties make a loose tie with green twine just below the bottom bud.

With some of the large standard cymbidiums, there is always the danger of heavy flower spikes breaking or bending under their own weight as the flowers develop, and they will need extra support from an early age. Where plants have more than one flower spike, these can be encouraged to develop in different directions, away from each other, so that they are as attractively displayed as possible.

If the orchid has several blooms, such as with paphiopedilums, cattleyas and lycastes, these should ideally be facing the same way. A paphiopedilum bloom should be left unsupported until the flowers have opened, then they can be tied individually to thin green canes inserted upright and close to the stems. Tie each flower to a cane; make one tie along the stem and a further tie immediately behind the flower so that the bloom 'looks up' and is not drooping. Cut off any surplus cane that protrudes above the flower. If some of the flowers are facing different directions, gently twist the cane with the stem tied to it, until all face the same way.

Cattleya flowers can be moved around on their cane in the same way, but the method of supporting them is slightly different. Use one cane for each flower. Cut a split in the top of each cane before inserting it into the compost, close to the flower. Open the split wide with

Phalaenopsis Brother Paul Valentine is one of many candy-striped, pink *Phalaenopsis* hybrids.

your finger and thumb, and insert the stem semi-vertically into it. The split will hold the stem firm and keep it in position. Now you can turn the cane to make the flower face where you want it to. Take care not to turn it so much that you snap the stem. Try to arrange the flowers so that there is not too much overlapping of petals, and each bloom can be seen fully. As well as showing off the flowers, this method will ensure that they do not damage each other, especially while being transported to the show.

When travelling with long flower spikes, insert an extra cane at an angle then tie the end of the spike to it to keep it rigid during transit. At the show, these travelling canes can be taken out.

Many of the smaller-flowered species require no extra support at all: their own natural habits cannot be improved upon. Remove all unnecessary string and supports at the show. These can always be replaced later, if required.

Damage

If a flower has become damaged with perhaps a broken petal or lip during transit, it can often be invisibly reattached or mended with a carefully placed thin strip of transparent sticky tape stuck to the back of the flower. An odd damaged bloom among many is best removed, so long as it does not lessen the impact of the remaining flowers. Some growers prefer to lay any broken flower parts at the base of the plant, to indicate that an accident has occurred.

PREPARING THE PLANTS

Ensure that your plants are clean and tidy. Remove all old bracts from leafless pseudobulbs, stripping them downwards one side at a time on cymbidiums, and carefully from around the base of the newer pseudobulbs with leaves. Any black tips can be trimmed to a 'V', and any old foliage that has become spotted or badly marked is best removed or reduced, along with any yellow leaves.

The leaves can be cleaned by wiping them with a horticultural wipe, available at garden centres. Do not use the artificial leaf shine that is manufactured for houseplants; this is not approved of for orchids. With long leaves, hold the base of each leaf and run the wipe along the length of the leaf. This will bring a healthy-looking gloss to the leaf. Be careful with young growths: their centre leaves can all too easily be pulled from their base. While you clean up your plants, check carefully for any sign of insect pests.

Make sure the flowers are in their prime. A spike of buds with insufficient flowers out may be disqualified,

Epidendrum pseudepidendrum var. *album* is a tall-growing, reed-type *Epidendrum*.

and any that are passed their prime will not be judged. Finally, ensure that the flower pot is clean and has been wiped.

Arranging groups

Where a group of plants are to be arranged together in a display, you can disguise the base of the plants to give the impression of a natural setting. You can cover the pots and staging with green moss, or pieces of cork bark and crisp beech leaves. Alternatively, you can cover pots and staging with black cloth, such as velvet, for an impressive base.

To create a display from a number of plants, first mark the centre of your staging area, otherwise you may find that after all is completed, the plants are noticeably off centre. Group your orchids in pairs, according to their size, height or colour. Any plant that cannot be easily paired can be used for the centre. Also reserve your best plants for the centre of the display. Begin to stage your group by starting in the middle of the back row, arranging the pairs of plants on each side, with the largest at the back and the smallest at the front.

Use stands where they are required. These can be clean pots or blocks of wood made for the purpose. When finished, one side of the display should balance and complement the other, with all the plants being as nearly as possible the same height on either side. This is the standard basic form of display. With experience, you can try more imaginative methods, incorporating your own ideas.

Some foliage plants can be incorporated to support the display, but this should not be overdone. A few small ferns placed in between the pots can add to the attraction. Other artificial props need to be kept to a minimum.

FINAL TOUCHES

Take care that no canes are showing where they are not needed. Be sure to label all your orchids clearly and accurately – apart from finishing off the display, this is a rule at many orchid shows. Keep the label as small as possible, using a white or green card supported by a wire stake, and place it as close as possible to the flowers. Write the plant's name in full, especially the genus. Remember that your orchids will be looked at by some people to whom the names may mean nothing. Abbre-

viations can be extremely confusing to anyone not familiar with orchids.

Make sure that you have read the show schedule and abide by the show rules. Nothing can compare to the disappointment of being disqualified through a technicality such as your exhibit being 15cm (6in) too wide, or your having one plant too many. If the show is to last for more than one day, give your orchids a good drink before leaving home and, when the work of staging is completed, syringe the plants lightly and, if you have used a natural base, dampen this. Of course, you should not wet velvet.

AWARDS

The major orchid-growing countries, which include Britain, the USA, Europe, Australia, Japan, S E Asia and South Africa, all have their own judging organizations – in Britain it is the Royal Horticultural Society, and in the USA it is the American Orchid Society. These organizations make various awards that are recognized throughout the world and are given to individual plants to recognize their merit. Such awards include the Award of Merit, the First Class Certificate and the High Class Certificate, listed as AM/RHS or AM/AOS and FCC/RHS and HCC/AOS. These letters are included after the name of any plant that has been so awarded, but these awards are made to individual plants, and no others can claim the award, even if they have the same name. Awarded plants are given further, varietal names to distinguish them.

Amateur growers can submit their plants for such awards, but it would be advisable to get the opinion of a member of the judging body (in Britain the RHS Orchid Committee) beforehand as to the quality of the plant to be submitted. Where a particular species or hybrid is a challenge to grow well and can be seen to have been exceptionally well cultivated, a certificate of cultural commendation is awarded to the grower. All this can make orchid growing far more exciting and give you a goal to strive for. In amateur classes rosettes are usually given, and these are eagerly competed for among members.

A beautiful flowering spike of *Phragmipedium* China Dragon benefits from a subtle support for its slender stem.

7
AN A–Z OF ORCHIDS

The orchids described here have been selected for their popularity among orchid growers. Consequently, they include some of the loveliest types, both species and hybrids, in cultivation. They have been placed in alphabetical order by genus. The hybrids illustrated are typical of their genus and are popular with amateur gardeners. Not all have an individual description. (Awards are noted, see p.60.)

As with all flowering plants, the orchid family is separated into tribes, and the tribes are further divided into subtribes. Within the subtribes are the genera, and these contain the individual species or hybrids. Here, each genus is introduced and the popular species are then described. After this, the most notable hybrids that have occurred within the genus are discussed, with the aim of giving an insight into the main breeding lines that have led to the present-day varieties. Finally, any intergeneric hybrids that have appeared within the related genera or subtribe are covered. As the term suggests, intergeneric hybrids are plants arising from crossing two or more different genera. This interbreeding of genera is possible with very few other plants (see also Hybrid Alliances, opposite).

Where many thousands of hybrids have been made, only those of exceptional merit are mentioned by name. If no mention is made, it is because little or no hybridizing has been carried out in that genus.

NOMENCLATURE
From time to time, orchids are reclassified. Where this has occurred recently, and to avoid confusion, such plants have been placed under the name by which they are most commonly known, and the name under which they are now classified is given in brackets.

FLOWER AND PLANT SIZES
The flowers of individual orchids are described as either small, medium or large. Small flowers are under 5cm (2in) across. Those considered to be of medium size are between 5cm (2in) and 8cm (3in). Flowers over 8cm (3in) are large. Sizes given for individual species are for young adult plants of flowering size. In time, many will grow taller or larger as they attain specimen size.

HYBRID ALLIANCES
Of all the orchids, odontoglossums, the largest and showiest members of their tribe, have been used the most for hybridizing. This started many years ago, at the end of the nineteenth century. In those days, collections consisted of species and the hybridist had a wide choice of the best plants to breed from and to pursue whichever colour line they wished – O. crispum and its enormous variations and different colour forms, together with O. harryanum and O. triumphans, offered a wonderful start to what was to become a fantastic range of colours and shapes.

It was not long before other related genera such as Miltoniopsis were being bred as well. Although the colour range is not so wide in this genus, there are many beautiful Miltoniopsis flowers, and their size and shape has been improved as well as their general quality. Spectacular colours vary from dark red to pink and white with yellows of pastel shades. The oncidiums have also been bred from since the begin-

Brassia Datacosa 'Coo's Bay' is a primary hybrid between B. caudata and B. verrucosa.

Wilsonara Widecombe Fair is an intergeneric hybrid, the
result of crossing *Cochlioda*, *Odontoglossum* and *Oncidium*.

ning of hybridizing, but not to the same extent as the
odontoglossums and miltoniopsis. Their main use is in
crossing with related genera to produce bigeneric and
multigeneric hybrids, taking advantage of their colour
and shape to enhance the progeny. With all these
multigeneric hybrids not only are there new generic
names, but also plants unlike any of their parents, with
completely new shape, colour and habit.

Intercrossing different genera was first done as long
ago as 1904, when a milestone was reached with the
creation of the first bigeneric hybrid, *Cochlioda
noezliana* × *Odontoglossum pescatorei* which, when
exhibited for the first time, caused a sensation in the
orchid world. The plant, which was called *Odontioda
Vuylsteke*, combined the size of the *Odontoglossum*
with the brilliant colour of the *Cochlioda*. While pure
Odontoglossum hybrids have been produced in their
thousands, *Cochlioda* has not been crossed with other
varieties of its own genus, but has been used extensively for interbreeding mostly with odontoglossum,
oncidiums and miltoniopsis.

Multigeneric hybrids involving four or five and even
six genera are now quite frequent, and today the range

is being made even wider with the intervention of *Aspasia* and *Brassia*, giving rise to yet more shapes and colours previously unknown.

Naming these intergeneric crosses produced another problem. When *Cochlioda* and *Odontoglossum* are crossed the result is *Odontioda*. *Cochlioda* and *Miltoniopsis* gives *Miltonioda*, and *Cochlioda* and *Oncidium* is *Oncidioda*, to give a few examples. But when a cross involves three or more genera, such as *Cochlioda*, *Miltoniopsis* and *Odontoglossum*, the hybrid is given a multigeneric name, in this case *Vuylstekeara*, after the originator of the first cross of its kind. Another example is *Wilsonara*, the result of crossing *Cochlioda*, *Odontoglossum* and *Oncidium*. These are only some of the intergeneric crosses achieved; there are many others.

The cultivation of intergenerics is very similar to that required by their parents. As nearly all have been produced from cool-growing species, general culture, as applied to odontoglossums (pp.120–121), for example, will suit them. The plants are often more vigorous than the parents and grow and flower quite freely.

When a number of separate genera are hybridized in this way, the resulting mass of new genera are referred to as an alliance. Hence the *Odontoglossum* alliance is used to describe any plant that has *Odontoglossum* blood in it. There are a few great alliances; the most important are the *Cattleya* alliance, which contain all related genera such as *Laelia*, *Sophronitis*, *Brassavola*, *Encyclia* and others, and the *Vanda* alliance, where again numerous man-made genera have been developed to create a huge group of related plants. In addition there are further alliances now being developed through modern breeding which include the *Zygopetalum* alliance and the *Phalaenopsis* alliance.

Apart from the alliances, there are many more orchids that will only cross-breed within their own genus. Paphiopedilums, phragmipediums, cymbidiums and dendrobiums are among the main genera.

THE PLANTS

ADA
Only one species of the 11 belonging to this very small but delightful epiphytic genus is in cultivation. The plants resemble *Odontoglossum*, with which they may quite easily be grown in the cool house, requiring the same conditions.

A. aurantiaca
This plant is shorter (15cm/6in high) and more heavily foliaged than the odontoglossums. The flower spike is produced in spring, from inside the leaf bracts, and carries a dense spray of small flowers. These are bright orange with narrow, pointed petals and sepals, and open only about halfway. This species has been used a little for bigeneric hybrids with odontoglossums.

AERIDES
Aerides is widely distributed throughout the tropical countries of south-east Asia, although the majority of plants in cultivation are from India and Burma. They are epiphytic and are found growing naturally upon trees close to water, often maturing into huge clumps making an impressive display when in flower and filling the jungle air with their perfume. The plants make extensive root systems, the long, white roots hanging down from the host tree and absorbing the moisture from the humid atmosphere. The genus name *Aerides* is derived from the Greek meaning 'air plants'.

The monopodial habit is typical of plants related to the vandas. Plants have an upright stem with leaves alternately placed along its length. The new leaves always emerge from the centre as the plant progresses upwards. Sometimes side shoots are produced, thus starting a new plant. The roots, which are thick, but brittle, appear nearly all the way up the stem. They are white with a green tip when growing. The flower racemes, which arise from the axils of the leaves, are usually pendent, carrying many medium-sized, very fragrant flowers. The sepals and petals are usually of equal proportions and waxy. The lip is comparatively large and is curious in that it usually has a spur that curves upwards towards the front of the flower. The basic colours of the flowers are pink and white.

Aerides may be grown in the intermediate house, where they enjoy shady, moist conditions. They are most suited to culture in baskets or, failing that, fairly large pots, when they may be grown in a coarse, open compost of well-drained materials, such as lumps of tree fern or bark. Once a plant has become established, it is better not to disturb it more than necessary. Owing to their complete lack of pseudobulbs, their only reserves are their thick, fleshy roots and leaves. Therefore they should never be allowed to become completely dry. As they very often make more aerial roots than pot roots, it is beneficial to spray them at least once a day and preferably more often during the summer months, care always being taken not to allow moisture to lie in the central growth for too long for fear of it causing decay.

A. fieldingii

This Himalayan species does not grow very tall. It has narrow, dark-green leaves up to 24cm (10in) long and coloured dark reddish-brown near the stem. The pendent flowering spike, which may be 30cm (12in) long, or more on a robust plant, is crowded with many fragrant flowers. They appear rosy-pink although the basal halves of the sepals and petals are nearly white. The large lip is pointed and a deeper but variable colour. This is an easy orchid to bring into flower; the blooms, which appear during the early summer, are long-lasting.

A. lawrenceae

A tall orchid, usually 1m (3ft) high in cultivation, though sometimes taller as a specimen. The plant is typical of the genus. The flowers are produced in summer. They are basically white, the sepals and petals tipped with rosy-purple. The centre of the lip is similarly coloured, and the upturned spur is yellow.

A. odorata

The habit and floral structure of this plant are very similar to A. *lawrenceae*, and although the flowers are extremely variable, they are generally creamy-white with more distinct markings. They are approximately 4cm (1½in) wide and are produced in summer.

A. vandarum

The habit of this species is quite different from others in this genus. The stem is slender and of considerable length, from 60–100cm (2–3ft) long. The foliage is cylindrical and well spaced, similar to *Vanda teres*. Large, very fragrant flowers, with narrow, twisted and wavy segments, are produced in twos and threes in summer and are about 5cm (2in) in diameter. The spur is very pronounced and the whole flower is pure white.

Hybrids

There are quite a few hybrids between *Aerides* and closely related genera, particularly with *Vanda*, making *Aeridovanda*. These hybrids are not plentiful and are, therefore, much in demand by collectors of the rare and unusual. One example of recent breeding is **Aeridovanda Norma's Fire Cracker** (*Aerides lawrenceae* × Vanda Dona Rome Sanchez). This hybrid has tall, erect inflorescenses of pink blooms with dark spots on the lip. The flowers are produced freely.

ANGRAECUM

This is a large and very beautiful group of epiphytic orchids, nearly all of the species being worthy of a place in any collection. Unfortunately, many of them are extremely rare. The species are distributed throughout the tropical regions of Africa and a few of its neighbouring islands. The plants are extremely varied in appearance from large, robust specimens with a vine-like habit to small individuals a few centimetres (inches) high. The blooms are usually waxy-white, with a tint of brown or green, and star-shaped, noted for their particularly long spur. The culture for these plants is similar to the warm house vandas and aerides.

A. distichum

One of the smallest of the angraecums. The broad, flattened leaves are closely set on the thin stem, which is barely 22cm (9in) high; the plant usually grows in a tangled cluster. Although slow-growing, the foliage remains for many years. The minute blooms are produced singly from the axils of the leaves.

A. eburneum

This species is found in Madagascar and on the mainland of Africa. It is a larger and more robust plant than A. *sesquipedale*, measuring well over 1m (3ft) from leaf base to leaf tip. The flowers are smaller and the nectary is shorter. There can be eight or ten blooms per spike and a mature plant will produce several spikes at a time.

A. eichlerianum

A tall, elegant plant with a flattened stem and a vine-like habit. The leaves are broad and about 7–9cm (3–4in) long. The flowers, about 7cm (3in) across, are produced singly and have thin, pale green petals and a large, spreading, white lip. Best grown on a wall or long wooden raft. Will not flower freely unless given sufficient light.

A. sesquipedale

This is a most remarkable orchid from Madagascar. The plant is large and robust, with leaves about 30cm (1ft) or more in length and up to 5cm (2in) broad. The flowering spike, which is usually produced in winter, bears 3–4 fragrant, long-lasting flowers at a time. The blooms are up to 18cm (7in) in diameter and the spur up to 30cm (12in) long. They are ivory-white, sometimes slightly tinted with light green. The fact that it produces large, white flowers with a strong perfume, only detectable at night, is a clue to its pollinator: a huge hawk moth with an extremely long proboscis. Most of the Madagascan and African angraecums are closely related plants. All have long nectarines and each has a specific association with a particular species of moth.

Hybrids

Hybridizing within the genus has achieved some spectacular results, but only a few hybrids have been produced. Attempts to cross these beautiful plants with *Vanda* from the other side of the Indian Ocean have been unsuccessful. The most notable hybrid is **Angraecum** **Veitchii**, a cross between A. *sesquipedale* and A. *eburneum*. This cross was originally made by Veitch in 1899 and is as popular as ever. Anyone collecting this group of orchids should include A. Veitchii, even though it can grow to 1m (3ft) or more in height. It has waxy, ivory-white, short-spurred flowers, 8cm (3in) across, which are produced on an upright spike.

ANGULOA

This is a comparatively small genus of about ten species, closely allied to *Lycaste*. They are found mostly at high altitudes in the Andes, and are mostly terrestrial. Robust growers, they produce large plants that make stout, oval pseudobulbs and carry a pair of broad, pleated leaves of a thin texture, which are sometimes deciduous.

The flower buds usually appear at the same time as the new growth, both developing together from the base. The flowers are borne singly on tall, upright stems, depending upon the species, and several spikes may appear at a time. The petals and sepals do not open fully but form a cup-shaped flower looking something like a tulip. Inside, encircled by the thick, heavy petals, is the lip, which is lightly hinged at the base, enabling it to be rocked freely to and fro when the flower is moved, giving rise to the popular name cradle orchid. The blooms are long-lasting and noted for their scent.

The general culture of these cool-growing orchids is very similar to that required by the more commonly grown lycastes, and this is covered more fully under that genus.

A. clowesii

This is probably the most popular of the anguloas, with large, fragrant flowers of a beautiful golden-yellow. Two, three or up to half a dozen spikes are produced on a specimen plant. This spring-flowering orchid, 60cm (2ft) high, comes from Colombia and should be grown in the warmest end of the cool house.

A. ruckeri

This species makes a slightly smaller plant. The outside of the large flower is yellowish-green, while inside, it is densely striped and spotted, although that differs from plant to plant. Flowering in spring or early summer, it is a cool-house species from Colombia.

A. uniflora (syn. A. *virginalis*)

The plant, 60cm (2ft) high, is typical of the genus, with tall, elegant foliage. The large blooms, produced in early summer, are white, delicately spotted and flushed with pink. Occasionally an albino form is seen, its flowers pure white. Best suited to the intermediate house.

Hybrids

Hybrids with *Anguloa* are, surprisingly, few and far between, and like the species are not difficult to grow and deserve more attention. Those hybrids that have been produced over many years are extremely beautiful. By far the greater number of crosses have been made with *Lycaste*, and probably the most exciting was the bigeneric cross between *Anguloa clowesii* and *Lycaste* Imschootiana, which produced **Angulocaste** **Apollo**, which, in turn, when crossed with *Lycaste* Sunrise, gave **Angulocaste** **Olympus**. These two hybrids have been highly acclaimed for their large, heavily textured, yellow and cream flowers.

ASCOCENTRUM

Only six or so species make up this very small epiphytic genus, often incorrectly placed with *Saccolabium* and widely distributed throughout south-east Asia. Those that are in cultivation are pretty. They resemble a miniature *Vanda* and the foliage is often spotted purple.

The culture is the same as required by the intermediate house vandas, but considerable light should be given if they are to flower freely. The flowers are small to medium, with sepals and petals of equal proportions, the lip small and pointed.

A. ampullaceum

This dwarf species, 15cm (6in) high, comes from the Himalayas. The flowers are produced from the lower half of the stem in short upright racemes of up to 18 blooms. Several spikes at a time may be produced in the late spring. They are deep rosy-pink, evenly coloured. This is an easy little orchid to grow.

A. curvifolium

At 30cm (12in) high, this is a more robust but rather straggly plant than the other two species described. It is easy to cultivate and will grow into small clumps. The flower spikes are produced from the axils of the leaves and the flowers vary from orange-yellow to tawny-brown. This is an excellent plant for mounting on bark or for growing in a basket, its flowers are produced at various times of the year: large specimens can be almost continuously blooming.

A. miniatum

A very charming little species from Malaysia and the Philippines. The stem is a little taller than *A. ampullaceum*, while the flower spike is longer, holding the small, bright orange blooms clear of the foliage in summer.

Hybrids

This orchid will breed readily with any closely related genera, such as *Vanda*. The resulting hybrids are popular because they produce compact, free-flowering plants with a wide selection of flowers. Among the most popular hybrids is **Ascocenda** Crownfox Moonlight (*Vanda sanderiana* × *Ascocendrum* Tubtin Velvet). The flowers have crystalline white sepals with yellow and green markings. Also popular is **Ascocenda** Gene Stevens (*Vanda* Fuchs Rosy Charm × *Ascocendrum* Yip Sum Wah), which has bright red flowers on upright spikes.

ASPASIA

This is another very small and not so well-known genus of epiphytic orchids from tropical America. They should be grown in the intermediate house and treated like *Brassia*. They are probably becoming more important today owing to their readiness to intercross with other genera such as *Aspasia* × *Oncidium*, making *Aspasium* and *Aspasia* × *Cochlioda*, making *Aspioda*.

A. lunata

The single small flowers of this species are star-shaped with narrow pale green petals, sometimes barred with chocolate-brown. The spreading lip is white, lightly marked with purple. The 15cm- (6in-) high plants produce a pair of oval leaves from the pseudobulb.

Hybrids

A. lunata has been crossed with various related genera, including *Brassia*, *Miltonia* and *Odontoglossum*. The results are heat-tolerant plants that enjoy tropical conditions. The intergeneric hybrids, even those containing genera that are not always warm-growing, are easily cultivated in tropical gardens, because the *Aspasia* influence produces a tougher plant.

BIFRENARIA

This is a small genus of attractive epiphytic orchids, the species of which are found mostly in Brazil. The plants produce hard, robust pseudobulbs with a single, stout, pleated leaf, 22cm (9in) long, carried stiffly erect. The flower spikes are produced from the base of the pseudobulbs. The flowers may be single in some species, or several to a spike in others; they are always fragrant and long-lasting. The plants do best placed at the warmest end of the cool house, where they should be given a decided rest when growth has been completed, after which the flowers will follow in the spring or early summer. During the growing season, they enjoy a moist atmosphere, although overhead spraying is not recommended because it can spot the leaves.

B. harrisoniae

The most common of the bifrenarias, this has medium-sized flowers on one- to two-flowered, short, upright spikes. The round, fleshy, creamy-white flowers have sepals and petals of almost equal size. The rounded lip is covered in short hairs, and is dark reddish-purple.

Brassia verrucosa (see p.70) has pale yellow-green flowers that are very highly fragrant.

B. tyrianthina

The habit of this species resembles that of *B. harrisoniae* when not in flower. It usually has more flowers to a spike, and they are larger and more highly coloured. The petals and sepals are shaded with rich rosy-pink, and the lip is deep reddish-purple; the colour may vary.

Hybrids

It is surprising that such an attractive genus has been so little hybridized. Although the scope is limited by the number of species, and the predominant colours are cream to pink, there should be some breeding opportunities for the enthusiastic hybridizer.

BRASSAVOLA

Although a very small genus, *Brassavola* is important for breeding intergeneric hybrids. Brassavolas are modest-sized plants that resemble a typical *Cattleya* habit, with elongated pseudobulbs bearing a single leaf. The large flowers are produced from the top of the latest pseudobulb; the predominant colour among the species is green. In their native habitat, from Mexico to Brazil, these epiphytic plants are found growing in thick clumps in fairly sunny positions on the trunks and branches of trees.

All brassavolas are best grown in the intermediate house. During the growing season, the plants benefit from abundant supplies of water, but once the season's growth has been completed, a decided rest is essential.

B. cordata

This plant bears long, pencil-like pseudobulbs that carry a round, solid leaf, 10cm (4in) long, pointed at the tip. The medium-sized flowers appear during the spring, in an inflorescence of up to six blooms. The star-like sepals and petals are pale green, while the heart-shaped lip is white.

B. digbyana (syn. *Rhyncholaelia digbyana*)

This species is by far the most important in the genus because of its contribution to intergeneric hybridizing. It makes a large plant 30cm (12in) high, resembling a *Cattleya*. The thick, stout pseudobulbs and foliage are blue-green. A large, single flower emerges from a large sheath and is about 10cm (4in) across and slightly fragrant. The sepals and petals are comparatively narrow and delicate green. The large lip is creamy-white, rounded and beautifully frilled. The species is most commonly found in Honduras and Mexico.

B. glauca (syn. *Rhyncholaelia glauca*)

More compact and shorter than *B. digbyana*, this species has large, solitary flowers of pale green with a white lip and pink stripes in the throat. It lacks the characteristic fringe of *B. digbyana*.

B. nodosa

A small species, 20cm (9in) high, from Mexico, with short pseudobulbs and cylindrical leaves. The medium-sized flowers are borne in threes and fours and can be up to 7cm (3in) across. They have pale green petals and sepals, with a contrasting white lip, and are long-lasting and often fragrant. The species has a wide distribution and can be found over most of tropical America.

Hybrids

All the species within this small genus have been used extensively for hybridizing, none more so than *Brassavola digbyana*. Its distinctive features, such as its huge frilly lip, have given so much to the cattleyas and laelias with which it is interbred.

The other species within the genus have also contributed much to their hybrids, particularly *B. nodosa*, which produces multi-flowered, pretty miniature hybrids; the flowers are unusual in shape.

BRASSIA

The brassias differ from the oncidiums, to which they are closely allied, in their very long, thin petals and sepals, which give the mostly large flowers a spidery effect. This, combined with their strong fragrance, accounts for their popularity. *Brassia* is a widely distributed, epiphytic genus, found throughout tropical America, and contains about 30 species. Most of these are easy to grow and free-flowering in the cool or intermediate houses, where they may be given similar treatment to the oncidiums.

Most of the brassia flowers conform to a basic characteristic shape, differing mainly in their colour and size.

B. elegantula

A dwarf species, 12cm (5in) high, from Mexico, with short foliage and small pseudobulbs, the base of the plant being shaded with reddish-brown. The small flowers are freely produced in the summer and are carried on a short, upright spike, no more than 15cm (6in) high, with petals and sepals about 2.5cm (1in) across. They are greenish and marked with brown bars, and the lip is white with a few spots. It should be grown in the intermediate house.

B. lawrenceana

This is a very striking species for the intermediate house. The plant is robust and bears long flowering spikes, 60cm (2ft) high, with well-spaced, fragrant flowers that can be very large – their narrow petals are up to 20cm (8in) long. The segments are golden-brown, spotted with reddish-brown. The heart-shaped lip is white with a few spots.

B. verrucosa

With more rounded pseudobulbs and stouter leaves than the previous species, *B. verrucosa* has long petals and sepals of pale yellow-green, darker towards the centre of the flower and largely spotted with darker green. The lip is creamy-white and spotted. It is also fragrant and is easy to grow in the cool house, appreciating a slight rest during the winter months.

Hybrids

Brassias regularly interbreed with one another as well as crossing with other, closely related genera. The most noteworthy *Brassia* hybrids are: **B. Rex** (*B. verrucosa* × *B. gireoudiana*), which produces long spikes of huge, attractive flowers in a delicate shade of yellowy-green, and **B. Edvah Loo** (*B. longissima* × *B. gireoudiana*), which has the longest petals of any *Brassia* hybrid. It is usually golden-yellow, depending on the clone. All *Brassia* species and hybrids enjoy strong light to induce them to flower. When crossed with allied genera, such as oncidiums, the plants are tolerant of high temperatures and can be grown successfully in tropical countries.

Intergeneric hybrids, such as **Beallara** **Tahoma 'Glacier'** (*Brassia* × *Cochlioda* × *Miltonia* × *Odontoglossum*), produce large, startling blooms, and can be grown and flowered in most climates. **Maclellanara**

Pagan Love Song (*Brassia* × *Oncidium* × *Odontoglossum*) is a wonderful orchid. On a huge plant, it can produce a spike well over 1.5m (5ft) long bearing large, dark green flowers with the spotted patterning characteristic of the *Brassia*. It would seem that the best hybrids are where the *Brassia* is most dominant.

BULBOPHYLLUM

Bulbophyllum is the largest genus of the orchid family, there being approximately 2,000 species. They are closely related to *Cirrhopetalum*, with which they are now considered to be synonymous, and are, therefore, included under the one name here. As might be expected, the distribution of such a huge genus is very wide, and indigenous species may be found in all the tropical and subtropical parts of the world, the greater concentration being in south-east Asia. They are epiphytic or lithophytic and their native habitat may be on trees or rocks, where their creeping rhizomes are attached firmly by the strong, wiry roots.

Basically, the plants are bulbous and carry a single leaf per pseudobulb. There any general similarity appears to end: one plant may consist of large pseudobulbs, the size of a man's fist, supporting a long, leathery leaf, while another can be so minute as to be overlooked at the first glance. The pseudobulbs may grow in tight clusters or spread widely on long, creeping rhizomes. However, nearly all bulbophyllums grow naturally in large, tangled clumps, producing many aerial roots, which are usually thin and wiry.

The flower spikes appear from the base of the pseudobulb, or sometimes from the half-completed growth, usually forming a cluster or rosette of blooms at the apex of the stem. This spike may be short, the flowers nestling among the bulbs, or tall and erect, holding the blooms clear of the foliage. The spikes may be one to many flowered.

The size and shape of the flowers is so varied that a typical form cannot be described. They are noted for having moving parts and in several of the species the remarkable sepals are elongated and taper to a point, while the small petals are often tufted with tesselated hairs, which quiver in the slightest breeze. The lip is generally very small and inconspicuous; occasionally it

Bulbophyllum purpureorhachis bears insignificant flowers on extraordinary flattened and twisted flower spikes.

Calanthe Gorey. Advances in the understanding of genetics have produced exciting new hybrids in a variety of shades.

may be fairly large and hinged lightly so that it will actually rock when alighted upon by a visiting insect. In some species the flowers resemble the open beak of a bird. They are often striped and spotted, and may differ from pure white to almost black, with orange, red, yellow and brown being the most prominent colours. Quite a number of them are scented, while others possess unpleasant odours. By far the greater number of species are very small and mainly of botanical interest.

The plants may be accommodated in the cool, intermediate and hot houses; it is difficult to give any general cultivation details for them all – a number of species have special individual requirements. However, most dislike too much disturbance at the roots, and these are best accommodated in baskets or shallow pans where they may be undisturbed and allowed to grow into large clumps, the rhizomes growing well beyond the rim of the pot. Their extensive root system will then become well established. They need well-drained potting compost, a fairly light position at all times and a decided rest during the winter.

B. barbigerum

An interesting West African species, 15cm (6in) high, with flower spikes about 18cm (7in) long, the small flowers being produced for about half their length, and numbering up to half a dozen. The sepals and petals are small. The lip consists of a mass of short, bristly, dark brown hairs that wave with the slightest movement of the air, giving the flowers a life-like appearance. Being a plant of tropical origin, it should be grown in the hot house. The flowering period is early summer.

B. collettii

This is a very attractive and free-flowering species, 15cm (6in) high. The flower spike comes from the base of the half-grown new pseudobulb; it grows to 10cm (4in) long and carries up to six long, narrow blooms. The dorsal sepal and the petals are very small and bear tufts of moving hairs. The lip is small and inconspicuous. The lateral sepals are held close together and are broad at the base, tapering to a fine point about 15cm (6in) long. The colour is rich maroon; the base of each of the sepals is striped with yellow. The species comes from Burma and will grow in the cool house.

B. dearei

From the Philippines, this species bears small flowers singly in the summer. Each has a large dorsal sepal and petals and lateral sepals of equal size. The lip is curiously hinged and is capable of turning upside down. The flower is very pale yellow, various parts being spotted and striped maroon. It should be grown in the intermediate house.

B. fletcherianum

This must be heralded as one of the giants of the orchid world. Huge, rounded pseudobulbs, which can be almost as big as a coconut, each produce a large, single leaf. Sometimes too heavy to stand upright, the plant will hang down by 1–1.5m (3–5ft). The whole plant is covered in a white bloom, such as you find on some succulents and cacti. Large, purple-reddish flowers are produced in a cluster around the base of the pseudobulb and have one of the worst smells of any orchid. The smell, which resembles that of putrefaction, can be detected from a considerable distance. For this reason, it is not the best of houseplants! This orchid is pollinated by carrion flies or wasps. Grow in the hot house.

B. guttulatum

The flowers of this Indian species are carried side by side on a 15cm (6in) stem, forming almost a complete circle and making an umbrella-like shape. The individual flowers are small, up to 2.5cm (1in) across, the lateral sepals curving inwards; the whole flower is pale yellow evenly covered with delicate maroon dots; the lip is more heavily marked. A single leaf, less than 15cm (6in) high, is supported by the rounded pseudobulb. This species quickly grows into a specimen plant. It is a cool-house plant, and flowers at various times, often twice a year.

B. lobbii

One of the strangest and most beautiful of the bulbophyllums, B. lobbii has round, egg-shaped pseudobulbs with a single leaf, 15cm (6in) long. The medium-sized flowers are borne singly on long stems. Each bloom is a large star-shape of yellow-brown. The lip is capable of rotating through many degrees as it provides a perfect landing stage for the pollinating insect. B. lobbii comes from south-east Asia and is best accommodated in the hot house, especially during the growing season. Mount on a cork slab or grow in a basket.

B. purpureorhachis

One of the most unusual of the African species, this is also one of the largest plants within the genus at 30cm (12in) high. The pseudobulbs are spaced well apart on a creeping rhizome and are flattened, or concave, on one side, and rounded, or convex, on the other. Usually, one or two stout leaves are produced on each pseudobulb. The plant is greeny-purple and the tall, upright flower spikes, which can be 50cm (20in) or more long, are flattened and twisted. The small, insignificant flowers are produced at intervals on both sides of the spike. They are a similar deep purple colouring to the plant. It flowers in the spring months in cultivation. Grow in the hot house.

Hybrids
B. Elizabeth Ann 'Bucklebury' AM/RHS (B. longissimum × B. rothschildianum). Long spikes, produced

from the base of the plant, bear several delicate, long-petalled flowers. The petals are fused together at the top and are pale to rosy-pink. Although correctly a *Bulbophyllum*, this plant was originally registered under *Cirrhopetalum*.

The very attractive **B. Jersey** (B. lobbii × B. echinolabum) produces one or two orangy-pink flowers on an upright stem.

CALANTHE

This is a large genus of very widely distributed terrestrial orchids, found from Africa to Australia, with the most important species coming from Burma, Thailand and Indo-China. Early orchid growers used calanthes for house decoration; large displays of well-grown plants created a beautiful sight lasting many weeks.

Calanthes can be divided into two groups: evergreen and deciduous. The latter are the most important, being by far the more showy and worthy of being grown. Anyone wishing to grow the evergreen types should cultivate them in the same way as that recommended for *Phaius*.

The deciduous species make stout pseudobulbs, up to 15cm (6in) long and sometimes waisted. These carry several ribbed leaves of a soft texture, which should be kept dry. The flower spike appears from the base of the completed pseudobulb. It varies in length, depending upon the species, but may be several metres (feet) long, and bears a head of medium-sized showy, long-lasting flowers. The sepals and petals are usually small, while the long-spurred lip is large and colourful. The flowers are produced in succession.

The orchids require annual repotting when the new growth appears in the spring. When root activity starts, watering is increased; by the height of summer, the plants should be receiving liberal amounts of water, so that they are continually moist, and should also be being fed with a liquid fertilizer. The new growth develops quickly and the pseudobulb is completed by the autumn, when the flower spikes appear and the leaves are discarded. At this stage, watering should be gradually reduced, until it is finally withheld altogether throughout the winter.

When the flowers have finished, the pseudobulbs may be removed from the pot, divided up singly after shaking off the old compost, and placed upright in a tray until ready for repotting. While the previous sea-

PLATE V

A selection of orchid hybrids

Vanda Vida

Dendrobium Utopia

Pleione Alishan

All flowers are shown at approximately half size

Ascocenda
Motes Tangelo

Vanda Motes
Buttercup

Phragmipedium
Eric Young

Odontioda Debutante
'Oxbow'

Paphiopedilum
Envy Green

son's pseudobulbs will produce new growths which in turn will flower, the oldest pseudobulbs usually grow again, producing a smaller flower spike for the first year.

Whether these plants are growing or resting, they should be given a sunny position in the intermediate house. With their short, fast-growing season, they enjoy high summer temperatures.

Hybrids

There are few, if any, *Calanthe* species in cultivation today. Among the deciduous calanthes, considerable hybridizing was carried out at the turn of the nineteenth century, when selective breeding produced a whole range of shapes, sizes and colours. However, interest waned and breeding was discontinued for many decades, with the result that the old stocks became heavily infested with viruses and were lost to cultivation. Renewed interest in the late 1980s and throughout the 1990s resulted in great strides being made. With an understanding of genetics and chromosomes, new shades from pure white to pastel pinks and very dark burgundy and with combinations of white petals and dark lips are being bred. New varieties are now appearing at orchid shows and in collections.

The evergreen calanthes have also received renewed attention, not so much in Europe and America but mostly in Japan, where the new colours are greatly prized.

CATTLEYA

This magnificent genus is without doubt the finest in this alliance which contains *Laelia* and *Brassavola*, among others. The species are striking for their richness of colour, large size and the fragrance of their blooms. In addition, they are easily the most widely grown plants in the orchid family, adapting themselves to varying conditions all over the world. In most countries they are grown in the intermediate house.

Nearly all cattleyas originate from South America. They are epiphytic or lithophytic, and grow on trees or on outcrops of rock, which makes them somewhat stunted. When established in their native habitat, the plants will live for many years, growing into enormous clumps many metres (feet) across.

The genus may be divided roughly into two groups: the unifoliates and the bifoliates. The unifoliate group consists of plants with club-shaped pseudobulbs, joined

by a creeping rhizome and spaced about 5cm (2in) apart. The pseudobulb and rhizome are covered in a white papery membrane, which is green in the new growth. At the top of the pseudobulb is a single, large,

broad, dark green leaf of a heavy texture. The flower sheath is produced from the base of the pseudobulb and consists of an oblong, pale green envelope that is almost transparent: through it, the flower buds can be

Cattleya aurantiaca (p.78) produces numerous small, bright orange flowers in summer.

seen developing, and, in time, will emerge to produce usually two large flowers. The bifoliates have taller and more cylindrical pseudobulbs that terminate in a pair of shorter leaves and carry more, although smaller flowers, of a heavier texture.

Cattleyas are best grown in the intermediate house, where they are so well known that this is often referred to as the cattleya house. They are easy to grow, thriving in warm, airy conditions, and should be given a liberal amount of sunlight at most times of the year, although during the summer, shading must be applied.

When the new growth starts in the spring and a new and active root system commences, watering can be applied regularly. In the autumn, when the pseudobulbs have made up and the root action slows to a minimum, watering should be reduced to allow the plants a slight rest.

Repotting, when necessary, is usually carried out in the spring, just as the new growth makes its appearance and before the new roots are active. However, these plants may go for many years without being repotted, and can often be seen with three or four pseudobulbs over the rim of the pot, while the plant continues to flourish and flower well. When repotting is undertaken, the rhizome should be cut with a pair of secateurs leaving approximately four pseudobulbs on the front division (see p.40). These may be potted up in a variety of different composts, so long as they are of an open, airy material and are well-drained. At the same time 'back halves' or pseudobulbs that have been removed may easily be propagated in sphagnum moss.

It is well known that cattleyas will withstand quite a bit of neglect, and do not attract red spider mite. However, they are very prone to attacks from scale insects, which build up their colonies unnoticed under the papery membranes of the rhizome and lower half of the pseudobulb. Such infestations should be swiftly dealt with by removing all the old sheaths as well as destroying the pest.

Cattleya hybrids often outshine the species, surpassing them in every way. For this reason, few of the species are found in cultivation today. Therefore, we have listed only a few to represent this very wide and beautiful genus.

C. aurantiaca

This neat grower from Guatemala produces slender pseudobulbs to 30cm (12in) high, with two leaves. The small to medium-sized flowers appear in large heads of up to 12 on a stem during summer. The sepals and petals are quite narrow and waxy, and the lip is unusually small for the genus. The flowers are self-coloured a bright orange-red. This species has produced some wonderfully richly coloured hybrids, among which *Laeliocattleya* Chitchat 'Tangerine' is probably best known

C. bicolor

This bifoliate species, 30cm (12in) high, comes from Brazil, where it grows at a high elevation on the trunks of the largest trees. The upright spikes carry 3–4 large flowers, usually in autumn. They have olive-green petals, brown-toned sepals and an unusual, reddish-purple lip.

C. bowringiana

Another bifoliate species, this time from Honduras. Also 30cm (12in) high, this was one of the most popular of the cattleyas, being very free-flowering with tall, slender foliage, but it is now rarely seen. The large heads of blooms with their rosy-purple flowers are a joy. The lip is a similar colour but darker. The petals can have a bluish tint about them.

The blue colour is quite pronounced in **var. coerulea**.

C. labiata

This species has many named varieties, together forming part of the unifoliate group. At one time many of the other unifoliate cattleyas were considered to be varieties of *C. labiata*, but today they are considered distinct species in their own right. The typical *C. labiata* flower can be as much as 15–20cm (6–8in) across with large petals of a bright rose colour. The broad, wavy lip is deep crimson-purple with a yellow throat. The flowers are long-lasting and very often fragrant.

C. mossiae

Generally considered to be a variety of *C. labiata*, this produces flowers that are usually a little larger with a more frilled lip.

C. skinneri

This species was originally found in Guatemala growing upon very high trees, making it difficult to collect.

It is similar to *C. bowringiana*, but is shorter-growing at 23cm (9in) high, and produces larger flowers which are carried in clusters. The petals and sepals are rose-purple with a deeper purple lip. In **var.** ***alba*** the flowers are pure white with a yellow blotch in the lip.

Hybrids

Hybridization within this genus has been carried out extensively for at least 150 years. There is hardly a species that has not been used as they are all beautiful. Not only will most readily cross with each other, but they are very successful in intergeneric breeding. There are many other genera closely related to cattleyas with which they will interbreed, resulting in combinations of six, seven and even eight different genera combined to make a fascinating man-made genus. When cattleyas are crossed with plants such as *Brassavola digbyana*, the lip is enhanced, making it bigger and more frilly. When crossed with the yellow laelias, brilliant-coloured petals are achieved, and when crossed with the miniature *Sophronitis*, bright red coloration is introduced.

Here are some of the more popular hybrids available today:

C. Winter's Lace is the latest in a long line of breeding of large, white cattleyas – in some cases the flowers can be as big as dinner plates. They are carried singly or in pairs from the top of the pseudobulb. The plants are robust growers, which gives them the strength to produce the long-lasting blooms. These can appear at almost any time of the year, but mainly during the winter months.

Brassolaeliocattleya **Pamela Hetherington** is a good example of the large, flamboyant, purple intergeneric hybrids of which there are many hundreds. The influence of the *Brassavola* gives the flower a large lip, and the broad, highly coloured petals come from the *Cattleya*. Little influence from the *Laelia* can be observed in this case. These magnificent orchids, which flower in the spring and summer, must be classed among the largest flowers and are always much admired on a show bench.

Sophrolaeliocattleya **Jewel Box** is one of a large range of miniature intergeneric cattleyas. Small and com-pact-growing, they are often multi-growthed and, as a result, can produce numerous flowers. The influence of *Sophronitis* has greatly reduced the stature of the plant and made it very free flowering. *S*. Jewel Box produces some of the finest dark red miniatures to be found. Other colours from this breeding combination can produce yellows and oranges.

CAULARTHRON

Only a single member of this very small, epiphytic or lithophytic genus is in cultivation today. It comes from Trinidad and Venezuela, where it is found growing in very exposed areas on trees and rocks. It is especially curious for its pseudobulbs, which may be 15–25cm (6–10in) long and are completely hollow, usually with a small split at the base.

C. bicornutum (syn. *Diacrium bicornutum*) In this species, the leaves are produced from near the top of the pseudobulb and the upright spike from the centre. On a strong plant this can carry 10–12 medium-sized flowers, which are of the purest white; the sepals and petals are of equal size and pointed at the tip. The narrow, pointed lip is peppered with crimson-purple spots and is yellow in the throat. The plant is 22cm (9in) high.

This species is best grown in the intermediate house on a raft or piece of bark suspended in a sunny position. During the period of inactivity a good rest should be allowed. Although beautiful, this is a somewhat difficult orchid to grow.

CHYSIS

Only six species go to make up this genus. All are handsome plants and their distribution covers a considerable area of tropical America. They are epiphytic with long, fleshy pseudobulbs, which are very thin at the base. The leaves are the same length as the pseudobulbs. In nature the plant usually has a pendent habit. Several large flowers are produced at a time, in a cluster from inside the leaves of the very young growth.

The plants are best grown in shallow pans or baskets, and hung in the intermediate house where a decided rest during the winter is necessary to produce flowers. While the plants need a sunny position, care should be taken not to overdo this to the extent of scorching the soft foliage.

C. aurea

This is a most beautiful species, 38cm (15in) high, found mainly in central South America. It produces long, club-shaped pseudobulbs which, unless supported, will hang over the rim of the pot or basket in which it is grown. The flower spikes can be 45cm (18in) long on fully mature plants, producing large, pale yellow flowers overlaid with a bright orange or brown patterning. A very striking orchid and well worth growing in the cool house during the winter. Give plenty of warmth and moisture during the fast-growing summer season.

C. bractescens

The beautiful flowers of this species are produced in spring. They have a waxy texture and are large, rounded and very fragrant. The sepals are broader than the petals, both being creamy-white. The lip is small and yellow with a few red lines.

COCHLIODA

Only a few species make up this charming little epiphytic genus. They are native to the Andes, where they flourish at a high elevation. Conditions similar to those that are required by *Odontoglossum* in the cool house suit them well; the plants closely resemble this allied genus. *Cochlioda* is best known for its great contribution to hybridizing. The species have been used extensively in making intergeneric crosses with odontoglossums, oncidiums and miltonias. There are only three presently in cultivation, and all of them are beautiful.

C. noezliana

A neat, compact plant 15cm (6in) high. The base of the leaves and pseudobulbs are reddish-brown, while the remainder of the foliage is dark green. The flower spike is arching and may be between 15–30cm (6–12in) long, carrying up to 12 brilliant flowers, often 2.5cm (1in) across. The slightly reflexed sepals and petals are orange-scarlet. The lip is the same colour with a yellow disc.

C. rosea

Similar to C. *noezliana* in habit, this species has small flowers of a more rosy colour, with a distinct white column, and the flower slightly smaller.

C. sanguinea (syn. *Symphyglossum sanguineum*)

The small flowers of this species, which do not open fully, are borne on drooping racemes, very often two to a pseudobulb and sometimes branched, when the plant is strong enough. A rosy-pink and evenly coloured, the buds at the end of the spike are the first to open. The plant is 9cm (3½in) high.

COELOGYNE

This is a very widely distributed genus with species being found from China to the Fijian Islands of the Pacific. Although this genus consists of well over a hundred known species, very few are in common cultivation. Those that are seem to be very popular. They are usually epiphytes, sometimes found growing on rocks. Coelogynes are bulbous orchids, mostly bearing a pair of broad leaves, the pseudobulbs joined by a creeping rhizome. The leaves usually persist for some years.

The species described below produce their flower spikes from within the centre of the young growth, and flowering is usually completed before the pseudobulb has made up. The one exception to this is C. *cristata* whose flower spike is always produced from the base of the pseudobulb.

The small to large flowers are borne in sprays, which may be upright, arching or pendent. The flowers are neat, the segments being equal in size, and the basic colour is usually white, although green, yellow and buff-coloured species do occur. While the buds of these orchids develop, they are covered in a protective sheath, which falls away upon blooming.

Coelogynes are both cool and intermediate house subjects, and most of them need a decided rest, after the season's growth has been completed and the plant has become dormant, if they are to flower properly the following year. In the spring, when the plants are starting their growth and flowering, water may be gradually increased so that they are wet at all times. The new growth at this stage is tube-like and will hold unwanted water only too easily. Care must be taken not to allow it to remain for too long in these new growths as this may cause damping off of the buds or spikes.

Repotting, which should only be undertaken when absolutely necessary, is done when the new growth is just beginning to show and certainly before the new

Cochlioda Floryi is a very old eyecatching primary hybrid that is still around today.

root development commences. Many of the species are most suited to culture in shallow pans or on blocks of tree fern.

C. barbata

A species for the cool house, this makes a robust plant with egg-shaped pseudobulbs, each bearing a pair of leaves approximately 30cm (12in) long and 5cm (2in) wide. The flower spike is erect and may produce up to six large flowers in succession. The petals are narrower

The pendent flower spikes of *Coelogyne flaccida* appear in spring and carry small, pale buff and white blooms.

than the sepals, and all are pure crisp white. The lip is brown with a margin or fringe of dense hairs. The blooms are usually produced in the autumn or winter, and last well.

C. cristata

This species is found over a wide area, although most of the plants in cultivation come from the Himalayas, where they grow at high elevations. It has been a great favourite for many years and is very often recommended as a beginner's orchid owing to its endurance of great extremes in treatment, although not always flowering freely without correct cultivation. The

plants (which are 15cm/6in high, but can spread to a metre/3ft or more) consist of tight clusters of round, shiny, light green pseudobulbs resembling grapes. The large, long-lasting blooms are produced in late winter or spring in drooping sprays from the base. Prior to opening, the buds have the appearance of being withered, when in fact they are quite healthy. Two to three flowers and sometimes more are produced; they can be up to 10cm (4in) across and are an intense crystalline white, except for a wide yellow streak in the throat. The edges of all the segments are crisped and waved.

There are two distinct varieties: **var. *alba***, whose flowers are of the purest white without any trace of yellow, and **var. *lemoniana***, in which the lip is marked with citron-yellow. In these varieties the pseudobulbs appear further along the rhizome than in the type.

This orchid makes very little root and resents repotting unless absolutely necessary. Therefore, it is best cultivated in large pans into which fresh compost containing some bark may be tucked between the pseudobulbs as required. Where possible the creeping rhizome should be tucked in as the plant grows. In this way it may remain undisturbed in the same pan for many years. After the season's growth is completed it is essential, if flowers are to be produced, to give this plant a decided rest, even to the extent that the pseudobulbs shrivel considerably. This is not harmful: they will plump up again when the growing season is recommenced. *C. cristata* does well in a fairly light position in the cool house.

C. elata

A large species whose stout, light green pseudobulbs are 12–15cm (5–6in) high and spaced 12–15cm (5–6in) apart along a creeping rhizome. The stiff leaves are long and broad. The erect flower spike is seldom taller than the foliage, and carries 5–10 blooms, 5–8cm (2–3in) across, with sepals and petals of pure white. The lip is prettily marked with yellow and orange. Because of its long, thick, woody rhizome, this plant is most easily accommodated on a branch or long piece of bark on which it may be hung up in the cool house.

C. fimbriata

A small but robust plant, 8cm (3in) high, which has the habit of always making two new growths from one pseudobulb, with the result that it can grow into large clumps. The individual plants are not big and can be easily accommodated in a small collection. The flowers are small and buff-yellow with a dark brown lip. They are produced in ones or twos from the new growth in winter or early spring. Grow in the cool house.

C. flaccida

An erect species with oblong pseudobulbs 5–8cm (2–3in) high, growing close to each other. They are dark green, bearing foliage of the same colour, and becoming ribbed with age. Pendent flower sprays are produced in spring, when the growths are very young. They bear 7–10 small flowers, 2.5cm (1in) or more across, of a pale buff colour, the lip white with orange to yellow in the throat. They are long lasting and very fragrant. This plant must have a decided rest in the cool house with plenty of light to induce it to bloom.

C. massangeana

This is a large, robust plant, 24cm (9½in) high, of typical coelogyne habit. The pendent flower spikes, up to 50cm (20in) long, bear many small flowers, about 4cm (1½in) across, with pale yellow sepals and petals of equal size. The lip is prettily marked with brown and yellow veins. A good grower, intermediate house conditions suit this plant best.

C. mooreana

A beautiful species whose pseudobulbs are borne close together and are light green and well rounded. The flower spike is erect carrying 6–8 large, drooping flowers, which somewhat resemble those of C. *cristata*. They have broad sepals and petals of a crisp white, while the lip is clearly marked with an intense golden-yellow. Like other cool-growing coelogynes, this plant should be resting when not in growth, but with this species severe shrivelling should be avoided as it will take a long time to recover. The variety **'Brockhurst'** FCC/RHS is even more beautiful than the type.

C. ochracea

A very pretty and sweetly scented species from India. It is a neat grower, the whole plant not more than

Coelogyne ochracea may produce several flowering spikes at the same time, making a wonderful display in spring.

20–25cm (8–10in) high, and can be easily accommodated in an 8–10cm (3–4in) pot. It will often produce several flowering growths at a time, making a lovely display in the spring. The small flowers are white, the lip marked with irregular yellow blotches each bearing a margin of orange. An easy-to-grow cool-house plant, this should have a place in every collection.

C. pandurata

A very striking species in which the pseudobulbs are large, stout and compressed, and are produced well apart on a thick, creeping rhizome. The two leaves, which are 45cm (18in) long, are very large and broad and the whole plant is dark green. The flower stems are produced in the spring, arching for about 60cm (2ft) and with up to 12 flowers, 10cm (4in) across, the sepals and petals a clear bright green. The lip is narrow and long, somewhat resembling a violin in shape. The crest is warted and veined with black, giving the plant its affectionate common name, which is black orchid. Found from Borneo to Malaysia, it is best grown in long baskets in the intermediate to hot house.

C. speciosa

This orchid has rounded, conical pseudobulbs, each bearing a single, dark green leaf. Plant 30cm (12in) high. The large flowers can be tawny-brown, with either a very dark brown, or sometimes pale salmon, lip. The lip is the largest and most dominant feature in this orchid, the petals being small and insignificant. The flowers are borne singly but the spike may produce up to two or three in succession. Grow in the cool house where it will make a specimen plant and flower freely at various times of the year.

Hybrids

For such a large genus, comparatively little hybridization has been carried out. This is largely due to the incompatibility of some of the species and their shyness to give fertile seed. The few notable exceptions are listed below.

C. Green Dragon (*C. massangeana* × *C. pandurata*). Long sprays of delicate green flowers, with an almost

The most conspicuous feature of the flowers of *Coelogyne speciosa* is the large lip.

black lip inherited from its parent C. *pandurata*, are produced on pendent spikes. For this reason it is best grown in a hanging basket.

C. Intermedia (C. *cristata* × C. *massangeana*). Although raised many years ago, this fascinating hybrid is still popular with collectors today. It has delectable long-lasting pure white flowers with lemon lips on pendent spikes. It is easily cultivated in the cool house, where it will flower in the late winter.

C. Memoria W. Micholitz (C. *lawrenceana* × C. *mooreana*) produces large, white flowers with a fiery orange lip. An attractive, cool-growing hybrid.

CUITLAUZINA

Once included in the genus *Odontoglossum*, only one epiphytic species makes up the genus *Cuitlauzina*. It differs mainly in the pendent habit of its flower spikes.

C. pendula (syn. *Odontoglossum citrosmum*)

A charming, sweetly scented orchid from Mexico, exceptional for producing long, pendent flower spikes. The plant, which is 20cm (8in) high, has shiny green pseudobulbs, each bearing a pair of leathery leaves. The spike appears when the new growth is very young, and immediately plunges downwards, growing at a fast rate to a length of 45–60cm (18–24in). It may bear 8–10 large, delicate pink flowers between late spring and midsummer.

Although not difficult to grow in the cool house, this species must have a decided rest during the winter, when it should be placed near the glass to ensure maximum light. Severe shrivelling of the pseudobulbs may be allowed, as the plant is subjected to this in nature, and it is, indeed, necessary to induce it to flower. In the spring, when the new growth appears, watering may be recommenced and the pseudobulbs will quickly plump up again.

CYMBIDIUM

The cymbidiums are, without a doubt, one of the most popular orchids in cultivation today, and are also the best orchid for the complete beginner. They are the most accommodating of cool-house orchids, withstanding a considerable amount of neglect and extremes in their temperature and general culture, in their turn rewarding the grower with long sprays of fine showy flowers in an abundance of different colours: white, cream or yellow to green, and pink, red and bronze, with every shade in between. The sepals and petals are of equal size – in a modern hybrid, the wider the better – while the lip is broad and coloured with contrasting, usually red markings, which may be spots, lines or a blotch. The flower spikes may be upright, arching, or pendent, and bear large blooms, with from six to maybe 20 or more per spike, depending upon the size of the plant and its breeding lines.

Closely packed flowers on a long, pendent spike are key features of the miniature *Cymbidium devonianum*.

In a well-chosen collection, the grower may have cymbidiums in bloom for over nine months of the year, the season commencing in late summer to continue throughout the winter with the mid-flowering types, and the later hybrids coming into their own by early to mid- or even late spring. The blooms will last for many weeks, although in fairness to the plant, it is advisable to cut the spike after the last flower has been open for about a week. The whole spray may then be placed indoors in water, where it will last just as long.

Cymbidiums grow into fairly large plants, making hard, round pseudobulbs bearing long, strap-like leaves. The flower spikes appear in the late summer, usually from the base of the leading pseudobulb, which has developed during the summer. Throughout the autumn and early winter, the spike slowly develops and when mature may be 1–1.5m (3–5ft) long. In the early stage, the flower spike can be distinguished from a new growth, which may appear at the same time, by its round, plump shape. A new growth is always flatter and within a short time divides into young leaves. As the flower spikes develop and grow, they will need a supporting cane, which should be tied in just below the buds.

During the summer, cymbidiums enjoy plenty of overhead spraying, several times a day, combined with plenty of water at the roots. At this time of the year, cool nights are essential and a maximum temperature of 10°C (50°F) should be maintained. If this is difficult, it is possible to place the plants outdoors for the duration of the summer, provided they are placed in a shady position and kept free from slugs and other garden pests.

Repotting will be necessary when the leading pseudobulb has reached the rim of the pot, on average every other year with mature specimens. The plant can often be returned to the same pot after the removal of a few of its back bulbs. These back bulbs usually start to grow after being potted up on their own, and thus may be used to increase stock.

It is the hybrids that form the greater part of any collection today, these having taken over from the majority of species. However, there are still a few species which can and do hold their own among the modern hybrids, and are worthy of a place in the greenhouse. The species may be epiphytic, lithophytic or terrestrial and are found from as far north as China to Australia in the south, from high up in the Himalayas to the coastline of the China seas, from tropical rain forests to dry rocky outcrops. The genus is very versatile and cymbidiums, with their varying habitats, have evolved into many different shapes and forms. The hybrids have been bred from only a small handful of species from the Himalayas.

C. canaliculatum

An Australian species, 30cm (12in) high, that does best either in the warm end of the cool house or in the intermediate house. When the growth is completed, it should be given a decided rest with plenty of light. The flowers are miniature and borne densely on the spike. Their colour is variable from olive-green to brown and in some varieties is a blackish-purple. It has been found in the wild, growing 5m (15ft) up on a dead tree, where the roots have penetrated down through the inside of the trunk to the ground.

C. devonianum

A cool-house miniature from the Himalayas; a most promising parent for breeding miniature hybrids. The plant grows to 30cm (12in) high but makes only small pseudobulbs with 2–3 broad, dark green leaves.

The flower spike appears in the late autumn and is in bloom from early to late spring. It is completely pendent – to the extent that, if one is not careful, it may bury itself in the compost. This is easily prevented by placing a small piece of label material just under it in its early stages to guide it over the edge of the pot. The spike will grow approximately 30cm (12in) long and produce a raceme of closely packed small flowers, the basic colour of which is olive-green overlaid with lines of purple; the lip is marked with diffused purple blotches.

C. eburneum

This species, 45cm (18in) high, has a long, narrow pseudobulb, and is usually heavily sheathed in foliage, the leaves being long and narrow, which is typical of Cymbidium. The 8cm- (3in-) flowers are produced late in the season on an upright spike, seldom more than two together. They are pure white with a yellow throat and quite fragrant. It is found growing at a fairly high elevation and is, therefore, suitable for the cool greenhouse.

C. elegans (syn. *Cyperorchis elegans*)

A moderate-sized plant, 45cm (18in) high, of typical cymbidium habit. The spikes are produced in the autumn and quickly grow and develop into an arching raceme of many closely set pendent flowers of pale straw-yellow. Slightly fragrant.

C. erythrostylum

A very fine, early-flowering species, 45cm (18in) high, that has helped to produce many of the pre-Christmas pinks. Although the spikes are short, several may be produced from a sizeable plant and there are 5–6 large flowers to a spray. The flowers are white, sometimes slightly peppered with purple dots on the basal half of the petals. The lip is creamy-white marked with purple. The two lateral petals point upwards, a characteristic that is carried forward into its hybrids. This Indian species is suitable for the cool house. Although scarce today, many of its fine hybrids are available.

C. finlaysonianum

This is among the cymbidiums best grown in the intermediate house. Its leaves are characteristic of the genus, but of a very much thicker texture. The species, which is 45cm (18in) high, is to be found wild over an enormous range from as far north as Burma through Vietnam, the Malaysian Peninsula and the Philippines, down to Java and Borneo. It usually grows on trees in sunny positions, where its long, pendent spikes bear many medium-sized flowers. Their colour varies, according to the locality, from yellow with a streak of red to a tawny-brown; the lip is usually similarly marked, and is blotched with a deep wine-red. The various colour forms from different parts of the world were at one time considered to be distinct species (C. *aloifolium* and C. *pendulum*) but are now generally thought to be synonymous. Surprisingly, little hybridization has been done with this plant, although it may prove worthwhile in producing hybrids to grow in hotter parts of the world.

C. insigne

Although almost unobtainable now, this species is included here as it was more common in the past, when it was well used as a parent: nearly all modern cymbidiums can claim descent from it. The plant is of typical structure. The erect flowering spikes, which carry 12 or more blooms, can be up to 1.5m (5ft) tall. The flowers, 8–10cm (3–4in) across, vary from rosy-pink to almost white, and the bases of the petals and sepals are heavily marked with red. The broad lip is usually darker with bright crimson markings. This is a very fine plant, and it is a pity it is so scarce today.

C. lowianum

One of the most popular species in cultivation, this orchid holds its place well among the modern hybrids. It makes a large, robust plant, 60cm (24in) high, and is capable of producing long, arching spikes of 25 or more flowers, each up to 10cm (4in) across. The sepals and petals are green, more or less suffused with brown, while the lip is cream, blotched with red. Originating from Burma, this plant does well in the cool house, flowering during mid- to late spring.

var. *concolor* differs in having greenish-yellow petals and a yellow-blotched lip.

C. mastersii (syn. *Cyperorchis mastersii*)

This species reaches 45cm (18in) high and has a tendency to be continually growing from the centre rather than having several pseudobulbs. The flower spikes appear, usually two or three at a time, from the axils of the leaves and carry 3–4 large flowers, ivory-white with a yellow throat, and very fragrant.

C. pumilum (syn. *C. floribundum*)

A dwarf species, 30cm (12in) high, from Japan, this orchid has narrow leaves and carries short, erect spikes of small flowers, which are reddish-brown with a yellow margin to the petals. The lip is white, dotted and marked with similar reddish-brown. A very pretty plant and suitable for the cool house. There are several named varieties of which **var. *album*** is a very pale form, while **var. *formosum*** is dark brick-red.

C. tigrinum

A dwarf plant, 22cm (9in) tall, with pseudobulbs like walnuts, bearing 2–3 broad leaves. Up to three large flowers are produced on a short spike. The petals are narrow and pale greeny-yellow with dotted lines of crimson. The hairy lip is creamy-white and is also spotted and striped. To flower this plant successfully, it is necessary to give maximum light and a complete rest after the season's growth is completed, to the extent that the pseudobulbs shrivel considerably. This will induce the embryo flower spike into activity. When this is seen, watering may be recommenced prior to the flowers opening in the spring. This orchid is a native of Burma, where it frequently grows on exposed rocky outcrops.

C. tracyanum

A strong, robust orchid, 60cm (24in) high, making large pseudobulbs with plenty of foliage, typical of the type. When not in flower, it can be recognized by the small, upright roots on the surface of the compost, appearing like miniature stalagmites. The flower spikes, which are at their best in the autumn, are long and semi-arching with 10 to 15 large flowers, the narrow petals and sepals are beige-yellow, usually with broken lines of crimson. The lip is hairy, creamy-yellow and spotted with reddish-brown. This is the most strongly fragrant of the cymbidiums.

Hybrids

The modern hybrids of today bear no resemblance at all to some of the less familiar species. It is mainly the cool-growing types that have been bred from, rather than the tropical or warm-growing varieties.

In the early days of hybridizing, it was always the plants with the largest flowers and best shape that were considered for breeding. Today, the novelty of a small, dainty plant draws attention, particularly for the amateur with only a small greenhouse. Hybridizers are starting to breed on new lines from some of the lesser-known and smaller species of the *Cymbidium* family, which hitherto have been regarded as unimportant. Through crosses of the miniature species with the modern hybrids, we are seeing some truly beautiful flowers in the second and third generation, in which the results in new shapes and colours are proving to be most rewarding.

Today, hybridization of cymbidiums continues apace and new hybrids are registered with the Royal Horticultural Society every month. Early hybridization was the province of British growers but now new hybrids are raised all over the world. While the early hybridizers created new varieties on a small scale, knowing that their customers would be willing to pay a great deal of money for them, today's new plants are quickly mass-

Cymbidium Red Beauty × Gorey is an attractive example of a modern *Cymbidium* hybrid.

produced by tissue culture, with the result that a global market is soon fulfilled.

Cymbidium hybrids can be divided into two groups: standard and miniature. Standard cymbidiums are those that have been produced from the larger species and where hybridizers have concentrated on flower size and vigour. It is within this group that the largest of the hybrids can be found – 60cm (24in) high, or more – with flower spikes 1–1.5m (3–5ft) high. The miniature, or compact-growing, cymbidiums are, as the name implies, shorter (45cm/18in high, or less), more compact and usually more floriferous, producing numerous spikes from comparatively small plants.

Standard cymbidiums

C. Red Beauty was first registered in 1979 and has since been used extensively for breeding. As its name implies, it produces very dark red, large, long-lasting blooms on upright spikes. It is important as a parent because it always improves the next generation, providing some beautiful reds and deep rosy-pinks through to soft pastel colours, which can be seen at orchid shows today. C. Red Beauty itself is now seldom found in cultivation, but its progeny are widely grown for both the pot-plant and the cut-flower trade.

C. Sleeping Beauty is a line of breeding that produces pure colours in the flowers. They are a type of *albino* or *leutino*, which means they are devoid of all colour pigmentation except yellow and green and the shades in between; even the lip does not have its characteristic red spots.

C. Solana Beach, originally from California, is one of the largest of the standard cymbidiums, producing huge, pale pink flowers, on tall spikes. The broad, spotted lip gives the flower a modern appearance. C. Solana Beach has produced some of the most wonderful modern hybrids. Its offspring are widely grown as high-standard pot plants and cut flowers.

Miniature cymbidiums

C. Darfield is a mid-season compact, extremely attractive plant with brick-red petals and a china-white lip which has a fringe of spotted patterning around the edge. This type of hybrid is very popular with the pot-plant trade as it takes up little room.

C. Maureen Grapes is one of the finest of the early cymbidiums bred to date. It bears tall, upright spikes of delicate apple-green flowers, each with a large, pure white lip covered in faint spotting. It has a strong perfume and when used as a houseplant will fill the room with its scent. On a large plant it can produce a series of flower spikes: as soon as one opens another will follow, extending its blooming over several months.

C. Summer Pearl, one of the earliest of the cymbidiums, flowering in late summer to early autumn in the northern hemisphere, was originally raised in New Zealand, and has now found importance as a summer-flowering pot-plant in Europe. The multiple spikes produce slightly fragrant white to pale pink flowers with delicately spotted lips. Due to their background, some of these early-flowering miniatures are not so long-lasting as the larger types.

CYRTOCHILUM (SYN. ONCIDIUM)

Members of this epiphytic genus produce large, robust plants with leafy pseudobulbs and thickened root systems. At one time they were included in *Oncidium*, but they differ in their flowering habit and the small size of the lip. No hybrids are in general cultivation and the species are scarce. They need to be grown in pots in a bark compost.

C. macranthum

From a high altitude in the Andes, this is an easy plant to grow in the cool house. The plants are large, 45cm (18in) high, and robust growers, with large pseudobulbs and plenty of foliage. The flower spikes appear in the summer and continue to grow over several months to a length of 3–4m (10–13ft). They have many short branches, each bearing 2–3 long-lasting flowers. The sepals and petals are club-shaped and of equal size; the petals are bright yellow and the sepals yellowy-green. The comparatively small lip is white with a purplish-brown centre. The large petals and small lip are a typical feature of these high-altitude plants. The long flower spike need present no problem in a small greenhouse, as it is very flexible while growing and can be trained into a hoop or circle between two supporting canes.

DENDROBIUM

This genus is considered to be the second largest of the orchids, consisting of approximately 1,000 distinct known species, and doubtless there are still a few to be discovered in the deep jungles of south-east Asia. Its distribution is enormous, from as far north as Japan and Korea right across parts of China to India, down through the Malayasian Peninsula and Indonesia to Papua New Guinea and the northern coast of Australia.

These orchids are sometimes found on rocks but are more usually epiphytic, growing in dense jungle habitats where they festoon the branches and trunks of their hosts, making a brilliant display of colour and filling the air with their strong fragrance when in bloom. Other species may be found on the most exposed parts of mountainous regions, surviving on scrubby trees or rocky outcrops, where their growth is usually tougher, adapting to its surrounding. All are noted for the daintiness of their numerous blooms, with pastel shades and delicate texture.

Due to the wide distribution and the variation in habitat and floral structure, it is not easy to provide a general description of the plants or their cultural requirements. However, the plant is basically a creeping rhizome which produces pseudobulbs that may be anything from 2.5cm (1in) high to 1.2m (4ft) – so elongated and thin that they are usually referred to as canes rather than bulbs – and in the wild develop a drooping habit. These pseudobulbs may be deciduous at certain times of the year, or evergreen. The leaves can be produced along the whole length of the pseudobulb or there might be just a pair at the apex. The small to medium-sized blooms may also be produced along the full length of the pseudobulb from the axils of the leaves, singly or in small panicles, or may appear in sprays from the apex. The lip is usually the most attractive part of the flower, often being deeply blotched with a rich colour. The sepals and petals are usually, but not always, equal in size.

It is not difficult to find dendrobiums that can be grown in either the cool, intermediate or hot house. In the spring, when the new growths start to appear on the cool-house varieties, watering may be commenced and every effort made to encourage the new growth by giving as much water as the plant will take (but not overwatering), together with fairly heavy shade and plenty of warmth. During the summer months, by which time ample new roots will have been made, the plants may be kept wet and constantly sprayed, as many of them have to complete a stem of considerable length in a very short time.

In the autumn or early winter, when the terminal leaf appears and the season's growth is completed, the plants will begin their rest, and will take a lower night temperature, combined with more light and less water. This will induce the leaves to fall and the pseudobulbs to ripen prior to the development of the flower buds. In certain species, if the rest has not been adequate, small plantlets will grow instead of flower buds. It is important, therefore, that during this period of dormancy, watering should be greatly reduced or withheld altogether, even though the canes may shrivel slightly; watering should not recommence until the flower buds or new basal growth start to develop. Full light is also essential at this time.

Where a cool and an intermediate house are available, many of the dendrobiums will benefit from being placed in the intermediate house, with its extra warmth and humidity, during the summer, and removed to the coolest and sunniest part of the cool house for the winter; others, though requiring the extra light during dormancy, are best kept in the intermedi-

ate temperature at all times. These extremes in culture reflect the long periods of drought, followed by equally long periods of continuous rain, to which they are subjected in the wild.

The compost for these plants should consist of well-drained materials. Compared with the size of the plant, most dendrobiums do not make an extensive root system: it is a mistake to overpot them, so the smallest pot possible should be used. Many of the dwarf types will do well in pans or half-pots, when they may be hung close to the glass and kept sprayed.

D. aggregatum (syn. *D. lindleyi*)

This short-growing species, 10cm (4in) high, has clusters of stumpy pseudobulbs, usually furrowed and wrinkled with age, with a solitary evergreen leaf growing from the apex. The flower spike, which appears from near the apex of the pseudobulb, is an arching raceme of deep golden-yellow, medium-sized flowers during the spring and early summer and is often fragrant. It is best grown in shallow pans near the glass in the intermediate house.

D. amoenum

A slender plant with long, thin pseudobulbs, up to 60cm (24in) tall, which are completely deciduous. The fragrant flowers are produced in ones and twos along the length of the newest bulb. They are small and white, the sepals and petals slightly tipped with amethyst. The lip is white with a green throat. This is a cool-house species that will do better if any extra heat and moisture are available during the summer, and a decided rest is provided during the dormant period. The plant is susceptible to red spider mite.

D. atroviolaceum

In this orchid, the hard, club-shaped pseudobulbs, to 20cm (8in) tall, have up to four broad, hard, evergreen leaves at the apex. The upright spikes bear up to 10 large, drooping flowers. The sepals and petals are creamy-white, usually heavily spotted with blackish-purple. The lip is pointed, and the side lobes are heavily blotched with violet on the inside, the outside being green. The flowers of this extraordinary plant will last many months in perfection. The species comes from Papua New Guinea and has produced a few hybrids. It should be grown in the hot house.

D. aureum

A short species, 15cm (6in) high, with smooth, deciduous pseudobulbs, the medium-sized flowers appearing in twos or threes from the upper part. The sepals and petals are creamy-yellow and pointed, the lip dark brown to amber-yellow. This is an Indian species and is suitable for the cool house.

var. *heterocarpum* is sometimes considered to be synonymous, but has taller, more slender bulbs; the flowers are larger but paler, otherwise they are similar. Both are very fragrant.

D. brymerianum

A beautiful semi-deciduous species with canes up to 60cm (24in) or more long. The medium-sized flowers appear in twos or threes from the upper part of the pseudobulb. They are 5–8cm (2–3in) across, with petals and sepals of a waxy texture, the whole flower being bright golden-yellow. The lip is the most won-

A very popular and widely grown *Dendrobium*, *D. nobile* has variable blooms each with a rounded, maroon-blotched lip.

derful among all the dendrobiums, being very large, and the greater part made up of interlacing filaments, forming a broad fringe.

This is a rather scarce species from Burma and Thailand. It should be grown in the intermediate house, where it flowers in early spring.

D. chrysotoxum

The furrowed pseudobulbs of this evergreen orchid are club-shaped and up to 30cm (12in) long. They bear 2–3 dark green, leathery leaves at the apex. During the late spring or early summer racemes of lovely flowers are produced from the top of the bulb, about 6–8 blooms loosely arranged on each spike. The medium-sized flowers are rounded and richly coloured in golden-yellow, the lip usually darker. A cool-house species requiring a decided rest.

D. densiflorum

A glorious species with erect pseudobulbs, 45cm (18in) or more in height. They are broad, square at the top, and bear 2–3 leathery leaves; sometimes, but not usu-

ally, deciduous. The flowers, produced in dense pendent trusses, have a soft papery texture, the sepals and petals curling slightly backwards. The large, golden-yellow blooms of this beautiful orchid unfortunately last only a week in perfection. The plant comes from Burma, is cool-growing, appreciating extra heat during the summer when possible. It will flower from old and new pseudobulbs.

D. falconeri
The pseudobulbs of this species are short – 15cm (6in) high – and thin, and branch profusely from the ends, forming long, dense, pendent growth. The plant produces many aerial roots and is best grown on slabs of tree fern or pieces of bark and sprayed regularly. If it can be hung over a water tank, it will benefit from the extra humidity. The bulbs are quickly deciduous, the grass-like foliage usually scarce. The attractive medium-sized blooms are produced in the spring; sepals and petals are white, richly topped with amethyst, the lip is coloured with rich dark maroon with two orange blotches. Cool to intermediate house.

D. fimbriatum
This well-foliaged orchid produces stout pseudobulbs, 60–120cm (2–4ft) tall, narrow at the base and semi-deciduous. Stunning rich orange-yellow, medium-sized blooms are produced in pendent racemes of 6–10. The lip is beautifully fimbriated, as the name implies.

var. *oculatum* has a dark maroon blotch in the base of the lip. It is far more common than the type. The plants will grow well in the cool house, flowering freely in spring, after being given an ample rest during the winter.

D. infundibulum
The pseudobulbs of this species are 25–50cm (10–20in) high, the top half bearing several dark green leaves, which may sometimes be deciduous. The whole pseudobulb and especially the new growth and young flower buds are thickly covered with short, black hairs. Large, exquisitely showy, long-lasting blooms are produced in groups of 2–4 from the top half of the previous year's pseudobulb. The flower vaguely resembles a cattleya: the sepals are narrow and the petals very broad and the whole bloom is pure white, except for the orange-yellow stain in the throat of the long-spurred lip. The plant grows well in the cool house, but can be included in the intermediate house for the summer.

D. kingianum
An Australian species with a very variable habit. The pseudobulbs are very broad at the base, tapering to a point at 25–50cm (10–20in) high and bearing 3–4 dark green terminal leaves. The spikes, which are produced from the apex, carry numerous small flowers that vary from almost pure white, through shades of pale pink to dark mauve and do not open fully. Although small, this is a very pretty species, enjoying dryish conditions with plenty of light in the cool house.

D. longicornu
A plant similar in habit to *D. infundibulum*, although the pseudobulbs are much thinner and more leafy. The long-lasting flowers, which appear in the autumn, are smaller, trumpet-shaped and drooping, the edge of the lip fringed with a few orange lines. This desirable, very free-flowering species is from Burma and grows very well in the cool house.

D. miyakei
This pretty species from the Philippines carries its striped, rose-pink flowers in tight clusters from the top of the older leafless canes. These grow upright to a length of 22cm (9in) and become pendent and curved as they age. The small flowers are seen at their best when the plant is suspended in a basket and allowed to droop. Flowering time varies, which allows the plant to remain in bloom over a period of several months.

D. nobile
Without doubt the most popular and widely grown of dendrobiums, this orchid is to be found growing wild over a wide area of India and as far south as Thailand and Vietnam. Those in cultivation today have usually been raised from plants of Burmese origin. The pseudobulbs are 45cm (18in) or more tall, stout and fleshy with broad, dark green leaves produced along the whole length; they are semi-deciduous in cultivation. The large flowers, which are long-lasting and sometimes fragrant, are borne in the spring. They arise from about halfway up the pseudobulb to the top, in panicles of twos and threes where the leaves have been shed. Blooms are extremely variable in shape and

PLATE VI

Odontoglossum hybrids and
intergeneric hybrids

Odontoglossum
Les Chenes

*All flowers are shown at
approximately half size*

Odontoglossum
Augres

Odontioda
Mont Ube

Odontioda
Plemont

Odontoglossum
Hautlieu

Odontioda
Bradshawiae

Odontioda
Bellozanne

Odontoglossum Tonto

colour: in the past there were several dozen named varieties. The typical colour of the petals is a pale rosy-pink, which deepens at the tips. The round lip is of similar colouring with a dark maroon blotch in the throat. Very few of the old named varieties are still available, but one that is still sought after by enthusiasts is **var.** *albiflorum*, which has a white flower with a maroon lip.

The plant may be grown in either the cool or intermediate house and needs a decided rest for the winter. Sometimes the season's growth is not completed by the autumn, especially on specimen plants with very tall pseudobulbs. In such cases, rest the plant as usual and recommence the growth in the following spring, otherwise there may be a lack of flowers for that season.

D. ochreatum

This is a short *Dendrobium* at 15cm (6in) high, the pseudobulbs curved and swollen at the nodes. This is a deciduous plant, requiring a decided rest when it is not growing. New growth appears in the late winter and develops quickly, the flower buds appearing from the axils of the leaves as the growth is completed, to bloom in the late spring or early summer. The small blooms are an intense golden-yellow, each with a deep maroon blotch. Cool to intermediate house.

D. phalaenopsis (syn. *D. bigibbum* var. *phalaenopsis*)

Native to Australia, this orchid produces fairly tall, woody pseudobulbs, 30cm (12in) high, with foliage at the top. The spikes are produced from the apex and may be 30cm (12in) long or more, carrying 5–10 showy blooms, often 8cm (3in) or more across. The flowers are highly variable in colour, from almost a pure white to rosy-pink and through to a deep rosy-mauve, while the lip is always much darker. The petals are rounded and the lip is pointed. Flowering time varies; grow in an intermediate to hot house, with a decided rest.

D. pierardii

This is an Indian species with very long, slender and pendent canes, up to 1m (3ft) long. It is most easily accommodated in a basket and is completely deciduous while resting. The flowers are produced in spring along nearly the whole length of the dormant pseudobulbs, often in twos and threes and each about 5cm (2in)

across. The blooms appear in spring and are very pretty with petals of a very delicate pink and the lip a creamy-yellow. It prefers to be grown as warm as possible to obtain the longest canes.

D. primulinum

With upright, thick and fleshy pseudobulbs, 23–30cm (9–12in) high, this species is completely deciduous, its foliage a soft light green. The medium-sized, very fragrant flowers are similar to those of *D. pierardii*, but the petals are rounder and appear in the late winter from the leafless nodes. Cool-growing.

D. spectabile

This plant is tall, 45cm (18in) high, with thick, woody pseudobulbs bearing 2–3 thick leaves, which remain on the plant for many years. The flower spikes are produced from the nodes between the foliage, and bear 6–8 large, curiously contorted flowers, the petals and sepals being long and tapering, twisting all ways and wavy at the edges. The lip is similarly contorted. The colouring is basically buff-yellow, streaked and veined with a dull reddish-purple. A rare but worthwhile species for the intermediate to hot house, originating in Papua New Guinea. It requires a definite rest when not active. Opinions vary as to the ugliness or otherwise of the flowers!

D. superbum (syn. *D. anosmum*)

Producing thickish pseudobulbs, 90cm (3ft) long, of pendent or semi-arching habit, this orchid is completely deciduous. The large flowers are produced from the leafless pseudobulbs in twos and threes in early spring. Long-lasting, they have long petals of a rich rosy-pink, the lip more pointed with a darker centre. Their strong fragrance is suggestive of rhubarb. It comes from the Philippines and should be grown in the intermediate house.

D. transparens

A tall species from India and Burma whose very thick, deciduous pseudobulbs attain a height of 75cm (30in). The medium-sized flowers appear almost the whole length of the previous year's pseudobulbs and are carried in small groups. The petals and sepals are pale pink, fading to white towards the centre. The lip is blotched with darker pink. This plant will produce a

Known as the blue *Dendrobium*, *D. victoriae-reginae* has beautiful flowers, marked and lined with purplish-blue.

good display of bloom in the spring, provided it has been given adequate light, in the intermediate house, during the resting period.

D. victoriae-reginae

A beautiful species, known as the blue *Dendrobium*. Reaching 30cm (12in) high, it may be grown upright in a pot or pendent on a piece of bark. The pseudobulbs are slender, swollen at the nodes, and branch considerably. They are generally deciduous. The small flowers are produced at various times of the year. The basal half of the petals and sepals is white, while the tips are coloured and lined purplish-blue. The lip is similarly marked. The flowers often do not open fully. Not common in cultivation, this species is very unusual and, being a high-elevation plant from the Philippines, does best in the cool house.

D. wardianum

A charming species that produces stout, fleshy pseudobulbs, 30–45cm (12–18in) high, with light green, deciduous foliage. The flower buds are produced in groups from the top half of the pseudobulb. The large flowers are white, the segments blotched at the tips with rosy-purple. The lip has a yellow disc, and two deep maroon blotches in the throat. A very long-lasting and good-looking orchid for the cool house. **var.** *album* is pure white except for the yellow disc on the lip; it is not so commonly seen as the type.

D. williamsoni

Similar in growth to *D. infundibulum*, but shorter, this species produces pseudobulbs with more foliage and covered in dark brown hairs. The smaller blooms are produced from the top of the pseudobulb bearing foliage. They have broad and pointed sepals and petals of creamy-white. The lip is pointed, with a brick-red centre. This scented and long-lasting species flowers in the early summer and is suitable for the cool house.

Hybrids

While there has been extensive hybridizing within each of the numerous different sections, little or no

Long-lasting flowers with an excellent shape are typical of
Dendrobium Pink Beauty.

hybridizing between sections has been achieved. *D. nobile* has produced a huge range of beautiful hybrids. Japan is leading this field, where growers have perfected the art of raising and flowering these orchids. The colour range is very large, from white, bright golden-yellow and pastel pink through to the deepest wine-red and any combination in between.

There is a section of dendrobiums that produce hard, bamboo-like stems anything up to 2m (6ft) high; an example is *D. gourdii*. They are widely cultivated in the tropics, where they flower continuously in full sun, giving wonderful displays, but seldom are grown in cooler climates, where they rarely do well, even under the best of greenhouse conditions. The *D. phalaenopsis* hybrids are related to them. Possibly the most famous of these is **D. Ekapol Panda**, grown in vast quantities for the cut-flower trade in Singapore and Thailand, from where the sprays are exported all over the world.

The Australian *Dendrobium* species have also been used to create new hybrids. These are more popular in Australia than in the rest of the world but where they are successfully cultivated, they produce a profusion of flowers.

D. nobile hybrids

D. Stardust is a delightful plant that will produce flowers the whole length of the stem. These are pale canary-yellow and appear in early to late spring.

D. Pink Beauty is a popular hybrid with flowers of excellent shape and long-lasting. They are delicate shell-pink with a yellow throat.

D. Thwaitesii An old-fashioned hybrid, but still popular today. Flowers with golden-yellow petals and sepals and a deep maroon lip are produced in abundance during the spring.

DENDROCHILUM

The species of this epiphytic or lithophytic genus are found over a wide area of the East Indies, but most of the cultivated plants originate from the Philippines, where they may be found growing on rocks or low branches of trees at comparatively high elevations. The plants are 24cm (9½in) high and produce small, oval pseudobulbs with a single leaf. The growth when young is heavily sheathed and produces its very thin and wiry flower spike in a graceful arch from the apex. The individual flowers are always small and partially closed, but on the dense spike produce a pleasing array of blooms arranged in two distinct rows, giving off a powerful perfume.

The culture of these plants is not difficult and most of them do best when grown in the cool house under shady conditions, never being allowed to become too dry at any time. Severe shrivelling of the pseudobulbs should be avoided, although less water will be required during their short resting period. Grow in pans, and cultivate into large specimen plants.

D. cobbianum

This species has small flowers densely packed in two rows down each side of a long, pendent spike. The colour is creamy-white with an orange lip. It flowers in the spring.

D. filiforme

The flower spike of this very dainty species is extremely thin and hair-like. It is sometimes called the golden chain orchid. The small blooms are star-shaped and canary-yellow. Well over a hundred contribute to make up the spike, which spirals delicately downwards, to charming effect, which is why the plant is given its common name. It is spring flowering.

D. glumaceum

This species is similar to *D. cobbianum*, but the spring flowers are usually less dense on the spike, the tips of the long petals turning upward. The flowers are a pale yellowish-white and strongly perfumed.

D. latifolium

This easy-to-grow plant reaches 22cm (9in) high with small, oval pseudobulbs and a single leaf. The new growth is very thin and hair-like, and assumes a drooping habit. The flower spikes emerge when the growth is still young. Small, deliciously fragrant flowers, neatly arranged in two rows, appear in early summer. They are creamy-white and last for up to three weeks.

DORITIS

This is a small, epiphytic genus of two or three monopodial species from India and Malaysia. The plants resemble *Phalaenopsis*, to which they are related and with which they will breed.

D. pulcherrima

A pretty, small-flowered species, 15cm (6in) high, with stiff, narrow foliage of grey-green, spotted with brown. The flowers, carried on an upright spike, are rosy-purple, with a deeper coloured lip. Flowering time is various. Grow this plant under the same shady conditions as the phalaenopsis in the hot house. Keep moist all year round.

Hybrids

Although a small genus, one species, *D. pulcherrima*, has contributed very much to intergenic hybridizing. When crossed with *Phalaenopsis* it adds a new dimension, increasing the richness of colour, shape and number of flowers per spike. The resulting bigeneric hybrid genus is called *Doritaenopsis*.

DRACULA

Grow these high-altitude, epiphytic Colombian species in the cool house in shady conditions alongside masdevallias, to which they are closely allied. Keep evenly moist, but not wet, all year. Originally about 80 *Dracula* species were included in *Masdevallia*. They were given their own genus in 1978. Although some of the flowers are quite grotesque, they nevertheless have an appeal, and are quite widely grown.

D. bella

This species has leaves that are 15cm (6in) high. The flower spikes are pendent at first, creeping across the compost in the same manner as a root. When the flowers open, they face downwards, and should be tied up to be seen to full advantage. They are large and triangular; the basic colour is white, densely flecked with brown; the long 'tails' are also dark brown. The small white lip is cup-shaped and loosely hinged. A succession of

Dendrochilum latifolium. Small, partially closed flowers with a powerful fragrance are typical of the genus.

bloom is produced from the spike, which should not be removed until withered. Flowers freely throughout the late summer.

DRYADELLA

This epiphytic genus grows on forest trees in Central America and Colombia. The species will grow in the cool house under the same conditions as masdevallias, to which they are allied. Grow in small, open baskets and keep moist all year.

D. simula

A curious dwarf species, 5cm (2in) high; the very small flowers are stemless, nestling among the short foliage, usually in quite a profusion. They are yellowish, heavily marked with reddish-brown spots. The lip is small and a dull purple.

ENCYCLIA

Encyclias are distributed throughout tropical South America, as far north as Mexico and the islands of the West Indies. They all conform to one type of growth habit: the pseudobulbs are produced from a creeping rhizome, round, oval or club shaped, with one or two terminal leaves. The multi-flowered spikes are produced from the most recent growth or pseudobulb and appear from the terminal. Their growing conditions vary considerably from cool to tropical, depending on their origins. In the wild they are mainly epiphytic.

E. citrina

A very beautiful, fragrant species, which grows downwards and is, therefore, more at home on a raft or in a basket. Its growth reaches 15cm (6in) long and it has round, clustered pseudobulbs covered in a papery bract. The single, large, lemon-yellow flowers are pendent and long-lasting. The petals do not open fully. This is a high-altitude plant that is best grown in the cool house.

E. cochleata

Large, flat, club-shaped pseudobulbs, narrowing at the base and terminating in a pair of dark green leaves, are typical of this species, which is 30cm (12in) high. The flower spikes are erect and may produce up to 10 large flowers in succession, the first being over before the topmost buds are open. The lip is carried uppermost,

and is white in the centre, covered with deep blackish-purple lines, which suffuse to become solid around the edges. The pale green and twisted petals hang down, like ribbons. It may be grown in the cool or intermediate house, where it will bloom freely at various times of the year.

E. fragrans

A widely distributed and very variable plant. The pseudobulbs may be 8–15cm (3–6in) high and compressed, and usually bear a single leaf. The medium-sized flowers, up to six at a time on an upright stem, are pale green or creamy-white. The lip is uppermost; it is

The arching multi-flowered spike of *Encylia linkiana* (p.102) carries many brown and white flowers.

rounded and veined with red on a white ground. It may be grown in the cool or intermediate house, where it flowers in the autumn or early winter.

Epidendrum pseudepidendrum var. *album* produces waxy, medium-sized flowers that last for several weeks.

E. linkiana

Among a huge genus of highly desirable species, this is one of the smaller, more compact varieties that takes up little room in a mixed collection. It produces small plants with a pair of narrow leaves to 10cm (4in) high. The small, brown and white flowers are produced in sprays. This orchid comes from South America.

E. mariae

This delightful species from Mexico grows at a high elevation, mostly on rocky outcrops. The clustered pseudobulbs and foliage are olive-green and the flower spikes are usually arching and can carry up to six flowers. These are long-lasting, and large for the size of the plant, which is 9cm (3½in) high. The thick petals and sepals are a beautiful lime-green, while the large, frilly lip is pure white. This orchid should be rested slightly during winter, and grown in the warmest end of the cool house, where it will flower during the summer.

E. polybulbon

A widely distributed species, most commonly found in the West Indies. A plant of dwarf habit, never attaining a height of more than a few centimetres (inches). The globular pseudobulbs are bright shiny green and bear two small leaves. A single, small flower is carried upright; the very thin sepals and petals are golden-brown, and in some varieties almost green; the large lip is almost pure white. In the wild this plant is found growing in the boles of trees or on rocks, the creeping rhizomes intertwining to form large mats several metres (feet) across. It is best potted in small pans and grown in the intermediate house, where it will bloom in the autumn.

E. prismatocarpa

The pseudobulbs in this species are stout and tapering, and bear a pair of long, narrow leaves. The tall, erect spikes are up to 38cm (15in) high and bear many medum-sized flowers. The petals and sepals are narrow, cream to pale green, blotched or spotted with purple, the small lip being rosy-coloured. A very pretty, fragrant and long-lasting species which will grow in both the cool and intermediate sections.

E. radiata

A plant similar in habit to E. cochleata, but the flowers are more like those of E. fragrans. They are beautifully fragrant, medium-sized and borne on an upright spike, anything up to 15 at a time. The waxy petals and sepals are thicker and more rounded than in E. fragrans, and the white lip is shell-like, lined with purple. Widely distributed throughout the Americas it is, therefore, variable; it will grow in the cool or intermediate house, flowering in spring and summer.

E. vitellina

A colourful Mexican species, 15cm (6in) high, in which the conical blue-green pseudobulbs grow in clusters. The flower scapes are up to 30cm (12in) long, sometimes branched. They bear medium-sized, long-lasting flowers of bright orange-red with a yellow lip. The flower shape is flat and even, the lip being pointed. It blooms during the summer and autumn. It enjoys rather dry conditions and should, therefore, be carefully watered during the resting period. Suitable for the cool house.

Hybrids

Hybridization within this genus has been practised for some time and intergeneric hybrids have also been created with Encyclia and Cattleya and other closely related genera. For horticultural purposes, the old generic name of Epidendrum has been retained. For example, where Encyclia has been crossed with Cattleya, the resulting hybrid is Epicattleya.

EPIDENDRUM

Species in this epiphytic, lithophytic and terrestrial genus are found all over the continent of the Americas, throughout the West Indies and out into the Pacific to the Galapagos.

Epidendrums produce their flowers from the top of the stems. Their vegetative habit is from small, about 15cm (6in) high, to tall reed-type plants taller than a man. Their flowers are even more variable, some bearing a single bloom at a time while others produce large, branched spikes. Or they may produce hundreds of flowers in continuous succession over a long period of a year or more. The colour variation and the combination of colours is almost without limit; every colour can be found: white, green, brown to orange and red. Mostly it is the species which are grown, little or no hybridizing having taken place. Being a genus of such wide distribution, it is difficult to give general cultural information for them all, but some may be grown in the intermediate house, while others may be accommodated in the cool house.

E. ciliare

This plant, which is 30cm (12in) high, bears a strong resemblance to Cattleya, with stout pseudobulbs bearing one or two thick leaves. Up to six medium-sized flowers are borne on semi-drooping racemes. Fragrant and long-lasting, they have petals and sepals that are very thin and a very pale green; the white lip is well divided into three lobes, and deeply fringed. It is a widely distributed species but most easily obtained from Mexico, and grows best in the intermediate house.

E. parkinsonianum (syn. E. falcatum)

In this species, the pendent rhizome produces a thick, dark green leaf from a virtually non-existent pseudobulb. One, or occasionally two, large, pale green flowers are produced from a thick stem. The lip is distinctly 3-lobed and ivory-white. The plant makes a multitude of aerial roots, and is best grown in the intermediate or hot house on a raft of wood, allowing it to hang downward, where it may attain a length of up to 2m (7ft). The species can be found all the way from Mexico to Panama.

E. pseudepidendrum

This reed-type species can attain a height of 60cm (24in) or more. The medium-sized, waxy flowers have narrow, green sepals and petals and a prominent, bright orange lip. The variety **album** has flowers that have paler sepals and petals and a yellow lip. Both come from Costa Rica.

E. radicans (syn. E. ibaguense)

One of the most popular among the epidendrums, this species can be found in almost every collection and is noted for its free-flowering habit and succession of blooms, which can last up to two years on a well-grown plant. It makes long, reed-type stems – specimen plants can reach 3m (10ft) high – with leaves carried alternately.

This plant will look its best when planted out and trained up a wall or trellis where, with its vine-like habit, it will quickly make itself at home, producing offshoots that propagate readily. The fine heads of flower are large, the individual blooms up to 4cm (1½in) across. The whole flower is evenly coloured bright red. The lip is carried uppermost and divided into three lobes, the edges of which are fringed. The individual flowers are long-lasting and when finished are replaced by a supply of new buds which develop from the centre. It will grow in the cool or intermediate house. This is the most widely distributed of all epidendrums in the wild, and therefore gives rise to several different colour forms.

EPIGENEIUM

This is a small but widely distributed and little-known genus of epiphytic orchids. Only one or two species are occasionally seen in cultivation, which is a pity as these are interesting and showy plants. The pseudobulbs are usually short and four-sided, of a hard texture and bearing a pair of short, stiff leaves from the apex. At the centre of the apex is the sheath from which the flowers are borne. The pseudobulbs may be spaced a considerable distance apart along a creeping rhizome, which produces very little root. For this reason, these orchids are best grown on long pieces of bark or moss poles, their culture following the same general lines as for dendrobiums.

E. amplum

In this species, the pseudobulbs are spaced 15cm (6in) or more apart on a long, upward-creeping rhizome. The large flowers are produced singly in the autumn when the pseudobulb has made up. The petals and sepals are of equal length and narrow and pointed. They are basically coloured pale green, shaded with brown or buff. The large, broad lip is white with a few markings on the basal half, the front lobe being deep brown or almost black. This interesting species from India does well when grown with the cool house dendrobiums.

E. lyonii

A showy species, reaching 45cm (18in) high, with clustered, cone-shaped pseudobulbs of yellow-green. The medium-sized flowers have thin segments and are produced in long, drooping panicles of a dozen or more blooms. The sepals and petals are rich maroon or reddish, paling to almost white at the tips. Although not easy to obtain, it is nevertheless a very handsome plant and well worth growing in the intermediate house. A native of the Philippines.

GONGORA

These epiphytic plants are found throughout tropical America, usually growing on trees in large clumps in fairly sunny positions. They have oval or cone-shaped, clustered pseudobulbs, normally becoming ribbed with age, which produce 1–3 large, pleated leaves from the top. The plants closely resemble stanhopeas, to which they are closely allied. The flower spike arises from the base of the plant, is pendent and may be up to 60cm (2ft) long. It bears numerous flowers that are curiously contorted to resemble a winged insect in flight.

These fanciful orchids should always be included in a mixed collection, and although their blooms seldom last more than 10 days, they are rewarding for their fragrance. The plants are best grown in pots or slatted baskets, hung in the intermediate house. They will flower more freely when given a rest during the period of slower growth.

G. atropurpurea

In the spring or early summer, this species, which reaches 30cm (12in) high, produces long flowering spikes that develop exceedingly fast. Each spike carries up to 30 or 40 small flowers and these are arranged symmetrically. The basic colour of the petals is creamy-white, heavily or lightly spotted with purplish-brown. The lip is usually a paler colour.

G. maculata

In this species, which is also 30cm (12in) high, the small petals are somewhat more pointed than in G. atropurpurea, and the markings are finer, giving the flower a peppered appearance; the actual colour of the flowers is also highly variable. This orchid flowers in the spring.

Gongora maculata has curious flowers with a peppering of dark colour on a lighter background.

HELCIA

There are only two species in this epiphytic genus. They come from the Andes, and are closely allied to *Trichopilia*. Their habit and culture, in a cool house, is the same.

H. sanguinolenta

The dull green pseudobulbs of this species, which reaches 15cm (6in) in height, are ovate and bear a single leathery leaf. Small, solitary flowers appear in early spring, several spikes at a time. The sepals and petals are of equal size, olive-green heavily marked and barred with brown. The broad, frilly lip is white with a few purple dots.

HUNTLEYA

This very small, epiphytic genus consists of plants with beautiful, star-shaped flowers, but only one or two are seen in cultivation. They are bulbless orchids, produc-

The flowers of *Huntleya meleagris* are heavy and waxy in texture with reddish-brown colouring.

ing tufted growths of a soft light green foliage, making very attractive plants. The foliage is delicate and is liable to spotting if the humidity is too high, or the foliage is sprayed too frequently. They should be grown in the coolest end of the intermediate house. Careful watering is needed: the plant should never be allowed to become completely dry, but at the same time saturation, which leads to souring of the compost, must be avoided, particularly if the root system is not very large.

H. meleagris

A very handsome species that produces several spikes at a time in the later spring or summer, each spike bearing a single bloom. The stems are approximately 15cm (6in) tall, and carry a large flower, with sepals and petals of equal proportions, about 7cm (3in) across. The base is greenish-yellow, gradually changing to a reddish-brown towards the tips, though highly variable in its markings. The lip is china-white, with reddish-brown at the tip. The whole flower has a heavy waxy texture, and is very shiny. The blooms are very long-lasting.

LAELIA

The genus *Laelia* is fairly widely distributed but is mostly found on the mainland of South America from Mexico to Brazil. The species are mainly epiphytic. The plants from the north have rather stumpy, short pseudobulbs, with long flower spikes, while those from the south are larger with shorter spikes, their habit resembling *Cattleya*, with whom they are closely allied and will easily interbreed. The flower spikes are produced from the apex of the pseudobulb.

The difference between *Laelia* and *Cattleya* is mainly botanical: the laelias have eight pollinia while the cattleyas have four. The southern species are best grown with the cattleyas in the intermediate house, while those from Mexico do well with the odontoglossums in the cool house. The compost should be of well-drained materials, such as chunky bark. When the season's growth is completed, these plants should be given a decided rest.

L. anceps

This is a very elegant plant from Mexico. The pseudobulbs are stout and four-sided, with a single rigid leaf. A tall flower spike, 45–60cm (18–24in) long, is produced with 2–3, or sometimes up to six, large flowers, which are 10cm (4in) across. The sepals and petals are soft rosy-pink while the lip is very rich crimson-purple with a yellow throat. This describes the typical form of this species, which varies greatly. At one time there were many named varieties that ranged from pure white to deep-coloured, but alas, few of these are seen today. This plant is best grown in the cool house in large pans and should not be repotted too often. In winter, rest in full light.

L. cinnabarina

In this species, the dark green pseudobulbs are narrow, wide at the base, and bear a single dark green leaf of the same size. The flower spikes are carried erect, up to 24cm (9½in) long with numerous small, graceful flowers of deep orange-red. It comes from Brazil and should be grown in the intermediate house.

L. gouldiana

A very fine orchid, generally considered to be a natural hybrid between *L. autumnalis* and *L. anceps*. The habit of *L. gouldiana* is more robust and the pseudobulbs are

taller and more rounded than in *L. anceps*. The flowers are large, deep rosy-pink, with a lip of even deeper colour. A very attractive autumn-flowering plant.

L. harpophylla

This plant is similar to *L. cinnabarina*, but the pseudobulbs and foliage are finer and more slender. The flower is more orange than red. Culture is similar.

L. majalis (syn. *L. speciosa*)

This species grows at high elevations in parts of Mexico. The clustered pseudobulbs are almost round and are wrinkled as a result of the very dry resting period it is subjected to in nature. Reaching 22cm (9in) in height, it is best cultivated in half-pots or baskets. During the growing season, it should never be allowed to become dry. The flower spike rarely bears more than one flower, but this can be up to 15cm (6in) across. It is fragrant, long-lasting and heavy-textured. Although variable, the sepals and petals are rosy-pink, while the lip is very large, rose-lilac and streaked with purple. This can be a shy flowerer, and must be well rested with full light during the winter.

L. milleri

A dwarf plant, 9cm (4in) high, from Brazil. The stumpy pseudobulbs are conical, bearing a single hard leaf of dark reddish-green. The flower spikes carry 5–6 blooms of a similar colour to *L. cinnabarina*, but the petals are usually wider and a much brighter red, the whole flower being evenly coloured. Grow in a half-pot or pan in the intermediate house.

L. pumila

A compact species of dwarf habit, 9cm (4in) high, for the cool house. The pseudobulbs are slender and carry a single leaf. The large, single, clear lilac-pink bloom is borne on a short stem; its petals are broader than the sepals, which overlap. The trumpet-shaped lip is blotched with a darker colour and yellow in the throat.

L. purpurata

One of the most outstanding *Laelia* species. Originally from Brazil, it has many variations and named varieties. The plants grow tall – 45cm (18in) high – and produce stout, club-shaped pseudobulbs with a single, long, dark green leaf. The flowers emerge from the

Laeliocattleya Gipsy Queen is just one of many beautiful plants produced by intergeneric hybridization.

previous season's sheath and bloom in the spring or early summer. They have large white, or pale pink petals with a prominent, trumpet-shaped, variable lip. The type is usually rich purple with yellow veining; however, there are salmon-pink, yellow and pure white forms, all of which are highly collectable.

L. tenebrosa

A stout, tall plant, 45cm (18in) high, with long pseudobulbs and a single, dark green leaf. Two to three flowers, seldom more, are produced. The reddish-brown sepals and petals are twisted, and lighter at the edges. This intermediate-house orchid flowers mostly in the late spring.

L. xanthina

A tall plant, 45cm (18in) high, closely resembling a *Cattleya*. It produces 2–3 blooms, up to 7cm (3in) across. The colour may vary from clear yellow to buff-yellow, except for the edge of the lip, which is white, streaked with crimson.

Hybrids

Since the beginning of orchid hybridization, laelias have been attractive to the breeder. The main species are capable of hybridizing and have been crossed within the genus as well as with allied groups such as *Cattleya, Sophronitis, Brassavola* and many others. The laelias are very diverse and have a great deal to offer to the breeder. The cool-growing species from Mexico, when crossed with plants from the more tropical South America, help to lower the temperature tolerance of the resulting hybrids, making them easier to grow outdoors in cool climates.

***Laeliocattleya* Canhamiana** (*L. purpurata* × *C. mossiae*)
There are hundreds of named varieties of *Laelia purpurata* in all different shapes and colours, resulting in this primary cross being made many times, giving a huge selection to choose from. Where the albino forms of the parents have been used, the progeny are pure white. Equally, where the blue forms have been used, the progeny are all blue. Primary hybrid vigour from such crossing makes the plants easy to grow. They retain many of the *Laelia* characteristics that are so admired in this genus.

***Laeliocattleya* Puppy Love** (*C. Dubiosa* × *L. anceps*)
Laelia anceps makes this a truly cool-growing, long-lasting hybrid. Usually 3–4 flowers are borne on the end of a long stem. They are a delicate shade of pink with a darker lip and a yellow throat. This plant can stand temperatures down to 10°C (50°F) on winter nights and in drier conditions even lower. *C. Dubiosa* gives the plant extra vigour and contributes to the fragrance, making an important *Laelia* hybrid.

LEMBOGLOSSUM (SYN. ODONTOGLOSSUM)

When the genus *Odontoglossum* was first described from a single herbarium specimen collected in the Andes, many fine orchids were included within the genus. Over the years, taxonomists have carried out much revision, with the result that nearly all the odontoglossums originating from north of the Panama Isthmus to northern Mexico have been reclassified into *Lemboglossum*. Older publications list these species under *Odontoglossum*. Most of these plants, particularly the true odontoglossums, have been hybridized between themselves or crossed with other species from South America. For hybrid registration purposes, the horticultural name of *Odontoglossum* has been retained, for example where *Lemboglossum bictoniense* has been crossed with oncidiums and odontoglossums.

For this reason we have discussed the hybrids more fully under the heading *Odontoglossum*.

Nearly all the plants in this epiphytic genus are cool-growing and well worth cultivation. *L. cervantesii* and *L. rossii* produce small, compact plants, easily accommodated in a small greenhouse.

L. bictoniense

A well-known and free-flowering species from Guatemala and Mexico, for the cool house. On a well-grown plant, three flower spikes may be produced from a pseudobulb. The upright racemes of flowers are 60–100cm (2–3ft) tall and sometimes branched. They bear many medium-sized flowers that are basically yellowish-green, heavily barred and marked with brown, the heart-shaped lip varying from white to rosy-pink. The flowers are sometimes fragrant. This is a variable species which had several named varieties, not common today. It is robust and easily grown, with pale green, delicate leaves and ovoid pseudobulbs. It needs little or no resting period and is liable to flower at various times of the year, but usually during the winter.

L. cervantesii

A pretty, dwarf species, 9cm (4in) high, also from Mexico, which does well in the cool house. The ovate pseudobulbs have a solitary leaf and resemble those of *L. rossii* in habit. It flowers in late autumn and will last in perfection for many weeks. The flower spike is semi-pendent and bears 5–6 medium-sized flowers of white or pale pink, each sepal and petal marked with a series of fine bars on the basal half, resembling a cobweb formation in the centre of the flower. The almost plain lip is white, with a yellow throat.

After the growth has been completed, the flower spike appears from the base of the pseudobulb. During the winter, before new growth appears in the spring, water should be reduced to give the plant a moderate rest. This species has several named varieties, which vary somewhat in colour; they are not often seen today.

L. cordatum

A distinct and handsome species, 15cm (6in) high, widely distributed from Mexico to Costa Rica and suitable for the cool house. It is recognized when not in flower by its flattish pseudobulbs. The spikes are erect or sometimes semi-arching, bearing many medium-sized blooms with narrow petals and sepals that taper to a fine point. They are yellow, blotched and barred with rich chocolate-brown. The pointed lip is white with a line of brown spots down the centre and another round the margin. The flowering period is spring.

L. rossii

Perhaps the most popular of the smaller-growing lemboglossums, this desirable little Mexican plant has small, ovate pseudobulbs, each bearing a single leaf. The long-lasting, medium-sized white flowers appear in the autumn on short spikes, 2–3 together. The sepals and basal halves of the petals are spotted largely with reddish-brown. The lip is heart-shaped, white or suffused with rose, often with yellow in the throat. It grows in the cool house, where it should be kept continually moist. **var. *majus*** is superior to the type.

L. uroskinneri

A showy and beautiful species from Guatemala and Mexico. The strong-growing plants have a creeping rhizome and shiny green pseudobulbs, which are sometimes spotted with purple. It is suitable for the cool house and should be kept watered during the winter. The large flowers, on upright spikes often 60–100cm (2–3ft) high, are chestnut-brown, mottled with green; the large, frilly lip is white flushed with rose. Long-lasting, they appear mostly in the autumn when the season's growth has made up.

LEPTOTES

This is a very small genus of miniature epiphytic plants originating from Brazil. Only two are found in popular cultivation today. These plants do best when grown in small pans or on blocks of wood suspended near the glass with the cattleyas where they will flower freely during the spring months, producing showy flowers, large in comparison with the size of the plant, which resembles a small *Brassavola*. The much-reduced pseudobulb bears a single, cylindrical, dark green leaf and the flowers are produced from the apex. Although the plants do not like to be overwatered, they should not be allowed to remain dry for too long.

L. bicolor

This is the larger of the two species, reaching 5cm (2in) high and bearing up to six flowers on a stem. The long,

PLATE VII

Oncidium species, hybrids
and intergeneric hybrids

Oncidium tigrinum
var. *unguiculatum*

Oncidium
maculatum

Wilsonara Widecombe Fair

Oncidium
Gower Ramsey

All flowers are shown at approximately half size

Ondontocidium
Russiker Gold

Miltonidium
Avalon Bay

thin petals are white, and the ends curl inwards slightly; the small, pointed lip is violet. Sometimes scented.

L. unicolor

Perhaps the prettier species with small flowers, half opening, of a very delicate rosy-pink, the lip of the same colour.

LYCASTE

This is a genus of showy and long-lasting orchids which are distributed widely throughout central America. There are a little over 30 named species in the group. The plants may be terrestrial or epiphytic and grow mostly at high altitudes. While varying in size, all produce dark green pseudobulbs that bear a pair of large, soft green, pleated leaves, deciduous in most of the species. The flowers are produced singly on a stem from the base of the pseudobulb, often 12 or more blooms at a time. In the typically shaped bloom, the sepals are large while the petals are smaller, often not opening fully. The lip is small in proportion to the rest of the flower.

During the active season, the growth usually develops quite quickly, and therefore the plants should be given an abundance of water, adding liquid fertilizer when watering. A moist, shady position in the cool or intermediate house will be suitable; ventilation may be freely supplied, but spray foliage sparingly.

In the autumn, when the growth is completed, the leaves often develop brown markings prior to dropping off. The plants should now be rested until the new growth appears in the spring. During this period of rest most of them will flower. At this time all water should be withheld and the plants kept in a slightly drier atmosphere, otherwise the buds may be affected by damping off.

Any *Lycaste* that starts its growth in the autumn, instead of the spring, should be watered throughout the winter and encouraged to grow, not forgetting that during the summer this plant will probably be at rest!

These are easy orchids for the beginner, being good growers that flower freely.

L. aromatica

The dark green pseudobulbs of this species, which reaches 30cm (12in) high, are rounded and flattened. When the foliage is shed, several thorny spikes are left on the top of the pseudobulb. The whole flower is bright orange-yellow and very fragrant. A native of Mexico for the cool house.

L. cruenta

With a habit and height similar to that of *L. aromatica*, this species has flowers that are usually larger, but not in such great profusion. The flower is bright yellow with a dark red blotch at the base of the lip. It grows in the cool house.

L. deppei

This orchid is also 30cm (12in) high. The basic flower colour is pale green, the sepals, which are long, narrow and sharply pointed, are densely peppered with reddish-brown, while the small petals are pure white and the lip is bright yellow with a few red spots. A very striking plant from Mexico, which comes into flower in the early spring. Suitable for the cool house.

L. skinneri (syn. *L. virginalis*)

One of the most popular of the lycastes, this species flowers during the winter. The beautiful flowers are very large, the sepals curling back at their tips. They are white, suffused to a greater or lesser degree with rosy-pink. The petals are heavily marked with deep rose spots at the base. The lip is white, spotted with crimson. **var.** *alba* has pure white flowers and is not often available. There are a number of other named varieties, seldom seen today, in which the colour varies greatly. Grow in the cool house.

Hybrids

Lycaste hybrids are plentiful and come in a variety of colours from white and yellow through pinks and orange, to dark red. When crossed with *Anguloa* to produce *Angulocaste*, the resulting flowers are often larger, and sometimes more richly coloured, including brown and green. Smaller-growing plants for the hobbyist are being bred.

L. Aubin (*L.* Balliae × *L.* Sunrise) First raised in 1957. A very wide range of colours from white, pale pink to dark pink and red. A large plant will have 20–30 flowers at a time and will stay in flower for two months or more.

L. Wyldfire (*L.* Balliae × *L.* Wyld Court) Large, dark red and, like all *Lycaste* hybrids, very long-lasting.

MASDEVALLIA

This large epiphytic genus of orchids includes natives of South America, and while a few may be found in Mexico to Brazil, the vast majority grow in the Andes, in the cloud forest regions of Peru and Colombia, where they thrive in the cool, moist atmosphere, growing on rocks or low trees. The plants produce solitary, thick, fleshy leaves from a short stem and do not have pseudobulbs. They very quickly grow into large, tufted clumps. The flower spikes, which may be as long as 60cm (2ft) or in some species much shorter, grow from the base of the foliage.

The flowers all have similar characteristics. The sepals, which form the main part of the blooms, are broad and often tipped with long tails. The petals and lip are very small and inconspicuous. Some brilliant shades of red are found in this genus, also soft browns and yellows, and one pure-white species. The blooms may be single or several produced in succession.

Cool-house conditions are ideal, the plants doing best in a shady position with plenty of fresh air combined with a moist atmosphere. They should be kept watered throughout the year and never allowed to dry out completely: being without pseudobulbs, they do not rest and should, therefore, be kept continually growing. Several new growths are produced at a time, and the plants are easily propagated by division. They look their best as specimen plants accommodated in shallow pans or, with some species, baskets: even a well-grown specimen does not need a great deal of room, and can easily be accommodated in an 8–10cm (3–4in) pan. A finely-sieved compost of bark will suit their fine rooting system.

M. coccinea

One of the most beautiful and popular of the masdevallias, this orchid has leaves up to 24cm (9½in) tall. The flower spike is much taller, up to 60cm (2ft) long, and produces a large, single bloom in which the bottom sepals are much larger than the dorsal sepal, forming a tube at the base that encloses the diminutive petals and lip. There are many named varieties of this species. They are all self-coloured, vivid and intense, and vary from a deep rosy-pink to blood-red as well as yellow

Recent advances in hybridization have led to the production of many new masdevallias, including M. Copper Wings.

and white. The species is from Colombia and usually flowers in the early part of the summer.

M. tovarensis

This species produces flower spikes 12–15cm (5–6in) high, which may bear 3–4 blooms at a time, flowering for two consecutive years. The blooms are of medium size, the two sepals larger than the dorsal sepal, all with fairly short 'tails'. The flowers are a powdery-white, and appear in the winter.

M. yungasensis

This pretty species from Colombia produces tufted plants that carry a single leaf from a basal stem and are

Overleaf: *Masdevallia yungasensis* bearing flowers with the 'tails' characteristic of the genus.

Maxillaria aracnita produces its numerous spider-like flowers in summer on a small-growing plant.

less than 15cm (6in) high. The flowers are whitish. They are produced singly on stems that are similar in height to the foliage, and they have the distinctive *Masdevallia* shape with the characteristic 'tails'.

Hybrids

The recent advancement in hybridizing has created a multitude of new delightful plants that provide an abundance of flower in a riot of new colours with striping and two-tone features on the sepals.

M. Angelfrost (M. *veitchiana* × M. *strobelii*) Bright orange flowers, 6–7 per plant, on long stems. They are comparatively large for the size of plant.

M. Hugh Rogers (M. *amabilis* × M. *yungasensis*) Of varied colours from peach to strawberry with darker stripes, this hybrid is extremely attractive.

M. Whiskers (M. *veitchiana* × M. *glandulosa*) This hybrid has dark orange flowers covered in purple spots with some striping.

MAXILLARIA

This is a large genus with something in the region of 300 species, widely distributed throughout tropical America. The largest concentration is in Brazil, where they mostly grow as epiphytes. The plants are highly variable: some are clustered pseudobulbs with one or a pair of leaves, others have small pseudobulbs and make small, creeping plants with grass-like foliage, while others have thick, leathery leaves and almost non-existent pseudobulbs. The flowers are always produced singly from the base of the plant. While many of the species are large and showy, quite a number are only of botanical interest. The flowers bear a close resemblance to those of lycastes and bifrenarias, and were at one time considered to be the same genus.

It is difficult to generalize on the culture of these plants as they are so diverse. However, the majority of species are not difficult to grow, and may be recommended for the cool house. A bark compost, similar to that for lycastes, will suit them well, but being epiphytes, they prefer a well-drained mixture. Many will be suitably accommodated in small pans or half-pots, suspended in a fairly sunny position close to the glass. A winter's rest is needed by most of them to ensure successful flowering.

M. aracnita

An attractive, small plant, only 15cm (6in) high. The plant blooms in the summer producing numerous, medium-sized, spider-like flowers singly on stems that emerge from around the base of the latest pseudobulb. The sepals and petals are white, very long and narrow, and the small lip is either yellow or orange. Grow this species in the cool house. After flowering, it will rest before making new growth.

M. grandiflora

Small, flattish pseudobulbs each carry a single leaf up to 45cm (18in) long. The flower spikes, 20cm (8in) long, bear a large, white flower about 8cm (3in) across. The centre of the lip is yellow and the sides are striped with crimson. This plant usually blooms in the spring and, being a high-altitude species from Ecuador, grows well in the cool house.

M. longisepala

This species has small, rounded pseudobulbs and grows to 22cm (9in) high. The extended sepals and petals are narrow, and may be 8–10cm (3–4in) long. The flower is translucent grey-green in the centre, fading to a soft pink at the tips. The smaller lip is pale yellow. This is an attractive species with its large flowers, though not always easily obtained. It originates from Venezuela and does well in the cool house.

M. picta

A very popular species noted for its strong perfume, which is particularly nice in the early part of the day. The pseudobulbs grow in clusters, are ribbed with age and have one or two strap-like leaves. A well-grown plant is 15cm (6in) high and will produce many blooms about 5cm (2in) across. The creamy-yellow sepals and petals are slightly incurving and heavily textured, and the petals are marked outside with reddish-purple. This

cool-house species comes from Brazil and may flower at various times.

M. sanderiana

The finest of the maxillarias coming from Ecuador, this species grows to a height of 45cm (18in). The flower spikes are produced almost horizontally, and the blooms may be 15cm (6in) across, with pure white petals and sepals, striped and spotted with reddish-purple, particularly at the base. The lip is similarly marked, with yellow in the centre. Unfortunately, this lovely orchid is scarce today.

M. tenuifolia

Small, rounded pseudobulbs are borne at intervals on an ascending rhizome, making this species a good subject for bark culture. It is 15cm (6in) high. The flowers are borne on short stems. The basic colour is yellow, the sepals and petals heavily marked and spotted with deep red. In some forms the red may become almost solid at the tips of the petals.

Mexicoa ghiesbrectiana (p.118) is a dwarf species with small flowers that have distinctive fiddle-shaped lips.

MEXICOA

This is a monotypic genus from Mexico. It was established from one small plant that was originally classified as *Oncidium*. There are several similarities with the oncidiums, and the plant can be grown in the same way in the cool house.

M. ghiesbrectiana

A pretty, dwarf species, less than 15cm (6in) high, producing small pseudobulbs with two leaves. The flowers appear on short stems from the base of the pseudobulbs. They are small, the petals and sepals are brown, edged with yellow, and the fiddle-shaped lip is yellow.

MILTONIA

This genus of epiphytic plants at one time contained many more species. Reclassification some years ago removed all the species, with the exception of the Brazilian ones, to *Miltoniopsis* or *Miltonioides*, leaving about ten true miltonias. Of these, only a few are in general cultivation.

Along with the miltonioides, miltonias are best in the intermediate house, unlike the miltoniopsis which are cool growing. Confusingly, miltoniopsis are still often referred to as miltonias, even for the purpose of hybrid registration.

M. flavescens

This pretty species from Brazil has pseudobulbs borne at intervals along a creeping rhizome which is often vertical and up to 23cm (9in) high, making it an ideal subject for bark culture. The pseudobulbs are long and narrow, bearing two narrow, pale yellow-green leaves. This is the natural colour and should not be mistaken as a sign of ill-health. The upright flower spike is 30–45cm (12–18in) long, and may carry 8–10 large flowers, evenly spaced down each side of the stem, in spring or summer. When the star-shaped flowers open, they are a very delicate pale green which ages to a creamy-yellow. They have a small lip marked with purple at the base. This plant should be given a slight rest during the winter, after flowering in the autumn.

M. spectabilis

This is similar to the previous species but shorter, with yellowish-green pseudobulbs at intervals along a creeping rhizome. The flowers are produced singly, or occasionally in pairs, and are extremely variable in colour, giving rise to quite a few very fine named varieties. The typical flower is large and flat; the petals and sepals are white with a tint of rosy-purple. The spreading lip is a much darker colour, and boldly lined. Summer-flowering.

Hybrids

M. Anne Warne (M. Bluntii × M. *spectabilis*) Sepals and petals glistening maroon-red; raspberry-red lip with darker veins towards centre.

M. Lucille Gibson (M. William Kirch × M. *cuneata*) Large, white flowers with heavy purple spotting mostly on the sepals and petals.

MILTONIOIDES

Miltonioides is a comparatively new genus, made up of plants that were formerly classified as *Odontoglossum* or *Miltonia*. The two species listed below have both been hybridized with either odontoglossums or oncidiums and therefore, for horticultural purposes, the older generic name has been retained.

M. laevis (syn. *Odontoglossum laeve*)

A very elegant orchid from Mexico, this species bears tall, branched spikes of attractive, fragrant, medium-sized flowers that are yellowish-green, banded and barred with deep chocolate-brown. The long lip is white, the basal half a rosy-purple. The plants, which reach about 30cm (12in) high, make large, compressed pseudobulbs with a pair of dark green leaves. They are free-flowering. This orchid is suitable for growing in the cool house and should be only slightly rested during the winter.

M. warscewiczii (syn. *Miltonia warscewiczii*)

This species is from Ecuador and grows to 30cm (12in) in height. It has long, flattened pseudobulbs, bearing stout leaves. The flower spike is erect or semi-arching, sometimes branched. It carries 6–8 medium-sized flowers which are usually clustered together. The narrow petals and sepals are brownish-purple, tipped white, while the sides of the lip are curled backwards to give it a roundish appearance; it is also dark brownish-purple. Spring- or summer-flowering.

Miltoniopsis, here the uncommon hybrid M. Lyceana 'Stamperland', has characteristic pansy-shaped flowers.

Hybrids

Odontioda Heronwater (*Odontoglossum laeve* (*Miltonioides laevis*) × *Odontioda* Memoria Donald Campbell) This hybrid has tall spikes, looking more like M. *laevis*, with some scent.

Odontonia Debutante (*Odontoglossum* (*Oncidium*) *cariniferum* × *Miltonia* (*Miltonioides*) *warscewiczii*) This hybrid makes a large, robust plant, with the vigour obtained from both the parents. It produces very large, branching flowering spikes with blooms that will last for a long time.

MILTONIOPSIS (SYN. MILTONIA)

Very few of the Colombian *Miltoniopsis* species are grown now, the beautiful showy hybrids having taken their place. The hybrid with which most people are familiar has a highly coloured, pansy-shaped flower with a large, flat lip and 'mask' of a contrasting colour. The most frequent colours found are rich dark reds, soft pale pinks and whites, with a few pale yellows, and every shade in between. The plants usually carry 3–4 large blooms on a stem and while these will last a considerable time on the plant, they wilt very soon after being cut and put in water.

The typical plant has the *Odontoglossum* habit but with more foliage and smaller pseudobulbs; the leaves have a soft texture.

M. roezlii

This plant has flat, pale green pseudobulbs which are well foliaged, with pale blue-green leaves, typical of the type. It reaches 23cm (9in) high. The short flower spikes carry usually two, large, flat flowers. The sepals and petals are white with a maroon blotch at their base. The broad, white lip is similarly marked with a bright yellow crest. It blooms at various times.

M. vexillaria

Resembling the habit of M. *roezlii*, this species has pale green foliage and many leaves to a pseudobulb. The flower spikes, often three to a pseudobulb, are tall and may carry six or more large flowers. They are pansy-shaped with bright rose petals and sepals, the lip a richer rose, whitish at the base and streaked with yellow and red. This colouring is typical of the species and may differ from white to dark rosy-pink in its several named varieties. From these different coloured varieties, many excellent modern hybrids have been developed.

M. Alexandre Dumas (M. Emotion × M. Brigadier) Yellow flowers, orange centre to the lip.

M. Lyceana 'Stamperland' FCC/RHS (M. Lord Lambourne × M. Princess Margaret) An uncommon, bicoloured flower: a white background with large, red splashes on all petals and lip.

M. St. Helier (M. Orkney × M. Alger) A strong pink flower with white edges and a maroon mask.

NANODES

This extremely small, epiphytic genus is very closely affiliated to *Epidendrum*. Two dwarf species can be found in cultivation under either name.

N. medusae

A high-altitude plant from Ecuador, this grows best in the intermediate to hot house. It is one of the most extraordinary of all orchids. The stems are flat and about 25cm (10in) long, and the fleshy leaves are set close together. The whole plant has a pendent habit, and should be grown on a piece of bark or a raft, where the heavy stems can be allowed to hang freely. Single blooms are produced, the petals being a greenish-brown, and the round, predominant lip purplish-brown and deeply fringed. The plant should not become too dry at any time, but kept in a shady position and regularly sprayed.

ODONTOGLOSSUM

The odontoglossums – species and hybrids – are among the loveliest of orchids. They were among the first to be cultivated and to enjoy popularity, due to their free flowering and ease of culture in a cool house.

The plants are compact: a mature specimen does not require much more than a 10–12cm (4–5in) pot. Almost without exception, they consist of a flattish, oval pseudobulb from the top of which is carried, either singly or in pairs, their dark green foliage, with two shorter leaves embracing the base of the pseudobulb. As the new growth is completed, the flower spike appears between the pseudobulb and one of the basal leaves. This will grow into an arching spray about 45–60cm (18–24in) long with numerous flowers evenly spaced down both sides. The basic ground colour of most of the pure odontoglossums is white or yellow with a yellow throat, and the petals and sepals may be heavily marked or overlaid with darker colours. However, the colour range and variations of marking are almost unlimited.

With a large collection of these plants it is possible to have blooms all the year round, particularly from the hybrids as they have no definite resting period and will flower when their pseudobulbs are made up, regardless of the season. A pseudobulb takes about nine months to complete so it does not necessarily follow that a plant will always flower at the same time each year.

The species of this delightful genus are epiphytic and originate from Central and South America; they are mostly found in Colombia and particularly on the westerly side of the continent. They are very much at home in the high altitude of the Andes, growing at between 1,800–2,500m. (6,000–8,000ft) in the cloud-forest regions, where the temperature is constant and the humidity always saturated. The plants will do best at the warmest end of the cool house, where a winter minimum night temperature of not less than 10–11°C (50–52°F) can be maintained. An ideal *Odontoglossum* house has plenty of fresh air and an even temperature, avoiding too much fluctuation, particularly on hot summer days. Keep direct sunlight away from the delicate leaves, for this can so quickly result in scorching, particularly in the early spring after long periods of dull weather. The humidity should also be kept constant, although too high a level during the winter may cause spotting of the foliage, particularly at the leaf tips, therefore copious spraying the foliage is not recommended.

Watering needs careful attention. Odontoglossums like to be grown in small pots, but this means they will dry out more quickly. The plants must be kept wet enough, otherwise the pseudobulbs quickly shrivel, and will take a long time to plump up again.

Place the plants on upturned pots or on a slatted staging to allow a free movement of air around them with adequate ventilation whenever possible. Odontoglossums like to be potted in a well-drained compost of bark, although the experienced grower will have success using a Rockwool-type material. Repotting is necessary about every other year, when the leading pseudobulb has reached the edge of the pot, and is best carried out after the plant has flowered and before it has started to make its new growth. The oldest pseudobulbs may be removed to leave a plant consisting of 3–4 pseudobulbs. Unlike cymbidiums, the chances of these old pseudobulbs making new growth are very slight, as any eyes have usually deteriorated with age.

To propagate an odontoglossum, where a plant is large and strong enough, remove the leading pseudobulb and growth, leaving the back half of the plant to start growing again. When this dividing is carried out on a strong plant, both halves will grow without any obvious sign of check.

When the genus *Odontoglossum* was first created, many plants from Guatemala and Mexico were included and there has been considerable hybridization between these and the odontoglossums from the Andes. Taxonomic revision has resulted in all those species from north of the Panama Isthmus being reclassified, leaving the only true odontoglossums in their high-altitude home in South America. For hybridization purposes, in such 'new' genera as *Lemboglossum* and *Miltonioides*, the older generic name is retained when naming the hybrids.

O. crispum

Originating from Colombia, this is a highly variable species and at one time some 200 varieties were known, their colours varying from pure white to pink-flushed, with plain or spotted petals, the lip similarly marked. Today, however, the genuine species is rather scarce, and there are more line-bred hybrids with large, round flowers that have wavy edges. These are crispy white with a flush of pink, especially on the reverse side of the petals. Apart from the occasional spot, the only other colour is the yellow throat.

This cool-house plant has no definite flowering period, and needs little or no rest. The usual green foliage may develop wine-red streaks when exposed to sunlight. This is not harmful, unless overdone.

O. hallii

This pretty species is from Ecuador where it grows at an elevation of 3,000m (8,500ft) and is, therefore, suitable for the cool house. The plant has oval pseudobulbs which bear two long leaves. The flower spikes are long and arching. The flowers are pale yellow with large, chocolate-brown patches and spots, the petals tapering to a point. The lip is white, marked with yellow and spotted and fringed. Spring-flowering.

O. pescatorei

A charming species, similar in habit to O. *crispum*, but slightly smaller with a branching habit. It was first discovered in the oak forests of New Granada at about 2,500m (8,000ft). The flowers, which usually appear between mid- and late spring, are white, shaded with rose; the white lip is spotted with rose and has a yellow stain in the throat. This is a cool-house species. It has several named varieties, all of them good.

Hybrids

From thousands of hybrids now available, the following are typical examples which represent the ability of these orchids to interbreed freely.

Odontoglossum Geyser Gold (O. Anneleise Rothenburger × O. Parade) This is a modern hybrid using O. Anneleise Rothenburger whose strong influence is from *Lemboglossum bictoniense* from Guatemala, and O. Parade, which is one of the hybrids descending from O. *crispum* from the Andes. The tall, upright, showy flower spikes are typical of this type of hybridizing. The flowers are pale yellow with darker gold markings from

Odontoglossum Hautlieu × Connero is a hybrid with self-coloured plum-red blooms.

L. bictoniense, while the larger flowers and more robust habit come from the other parent. This plant has been extensively tissue-cultured and is now widely available from most orchid nurseries or as a pot plant.

Odontocidium Purbeck Gold (*Oncidium tigrinum* × *Odontoglossum* Gold Cup) The Mexican *Oncidium tigrinum* has contributed greatly to the hybridizing of odontoglossums. This cross with a hybrid from South America retains the vigour, large pseudobulbs and bright golden-yellow of the *Oncidium*, while the *Odontoglossum* contributes shape and size of bloom. The result is an attractive golden-yellow lip with the sepals and petals barred in chestnut-brown. Some yellow *Odontoglossum* hybrids fade after a few weeks but this variety holds its colour well.

Vuylstekeara Monica 'Burnham' (*V.* Aspasia × *Odontioda* Colombia) A trigeneric hybrid within this family is a good example of some of the early breeding.

It was carried out as long ago as the 1930s but is still popular today and sought after by collectors of the unusual. The flower spikes are of medium height with dark purple flowers, a somewhat unusual colour in the *Odontoglossum* family.

OERSTEDELLA

This is a genus of about 40 mainly small-growing, epiphytic or terrestrial plants from Mexico, which were at one time contained in the genus *Epidendrum*. Although they are mostly pretty, very few are in general cultivation. They have cane-like, leafy stems, and flower from the apex when the season's growth is matured. The plants do best in the intermediate house or the warmest end of the cool house, where they should be kept watered throughout the year, with less water in winter.

O. centradenia

This attractive species produces slender foliage on slender canes that can be up to 15cm (6in) or more in height. The clusters of flowers emerge from the apex of the cane during the summer. The plant comes from

Costa Rica and needs to be grown in the intermediate house in summer, and rested in winter.

ONCIDIUM

This is a beautiful genus with a wide range of habit, colour and inflorescence style. The species are found in the Americas, from as far north as the southern states of the USA, to all tropical American countries down to Argentina, as well as many of the islands of the West Indies. They grow from sea-level to high in the Andes, and from the dry, almost desert conditions of Mexico, to the tropical rain forests of Brazil, adapting themselves to every environment; there are both epiphytic and lithophytic types. They have produced many strange and different forms to make up one of the largest genera of orchids: there are over 400 known species. Many of them will grow in the cool greenhouse alongside the odontoglossums, requiring similar treatment. Others need to be grown in the intermediate or hot house, where they benefit from the extra warmth, but often require a lot more light to induce them to flower.

O. aureum

One of the high-altitude species, mainly from Ecuador, this orchid has soft green foliage and pale green pseudobulbs, and makes a plant 45cm (18in) high. The flower spikes are tall and erect, and sometimes branched. They bear several small, bright canary-yellow flowers of a waxy texture. The sepals, petals and pointed lip are all of similar size. The flowering period is usually spring. It grows well in the cool house.

O. cebolleta

The almost non-existent pseudobulbs of this species, which grows to 23cm (9in) high, bear a large, cylindrical, dark green leaf. This grows erect to a sharp point and has a very hard surface. The flower spike is about 45cm (18in) high, sometimes branched, and carries several flowers with predominantly bright yellow lips. The smaller sepals and petals are marked with brown. Being a widely distributed species, it is quite variable in flowers and habit. It should be grown in the intermediate house, where it will flower during the summer.

O. cheirophorum

A pretty, dwarf species, 10cm (4in) high, from Colombia which carries flower spikes with small, dense, bright yellow flowers that are sweetly fragrant. Several spikes can be expected from each of the small, clustered pseudobulbs. Suitable for the cool house, it flowers during the autumn.

O. concolor

One of the most attractive of the yellow-flowered species, this oncidium is quite small at 15cm (6in) high. The 6–8 large flowers are borne on a drooping spike, their main feature being the large lemon-yellow lip. The sepals and petals are very small in comparison and embrace the column. The plant has fairly small, dark green pseudobulbs with a pair of dark green leaves. A cool-growing plant, it flowers in the early summer, requires a slight rest during the winter and is sometimes slow to recommence new growth.

O. crispum

A remarkably handsome and large-flowered species from Brazil. The pseudobulbs and foliage are attractive green-brown. The plant reaches 30cm (12in) high. The tall, branched flower spikes carry up to a dozen large flowers. The individual blooms are golden-brown with a yellow margin and yellow in the throat. This cool-growing species flowers at various times of the year.

O. cucullatum

This cool-house species comes from a high elevation mainly in Ecuador and makes a plant 15cm (6in) high. The flower spikes are produced in the spring, and the flowers will last a long time in perfection. The colours are variable, from plum-purple to chestnut-brown, while the lip may be rosy-purple and spotted. There are several named varieties, which include **var. *nubigenum***, which has a much smaller flower with an almost white lip, and **var. *phalaenopsis***, which has a much paler flower with purple blotches.

O. flexuosum

One of the most popular of the small-flowered oncidiums, this species is 30cm (12in) or more high and may be grown and flowered in the cool house. The pale green pseudobulbs are widely spaced along a creeping or upright rhizome, which may be more easily accommodated on a piece of bark than in a pot. The flower spikes can be 45–60cm (18–24in) long and are produced at various times of the year. They carry a dense mass of small brightly coloured yellow flowers. The smaller sepals and petals are barred with reddish-brown.

O. hastatum

The pseudobulbs in this species are round and firm. They grow in clusters, making a plant 23cm (9in) high, and produce a tall flower spike, 90cm–1.2m (3–4ft) high, that branches at right angles to the stem. The flowers are 3–5cm (1–2in) across, the sepals and petals narrow, pale olive-green and lightly marked with brown. The fairly small, white lip has a dark pink centre. This is a cool-house species that flowers in spring and early summer.

O. incurvum

The pseudobulbs of this pretty species, which is 23cm (9in) high, are short, rounded and slightly ribbed, while the flower spikes are tall, 1–2m (3–6ft) or more, taking on a graceful arch as they grow and bearing many branches that can easily carry over 100 elegant, small, sweetly fragrant flowers. The petals and sepals, which are thin and twisted, are white, heavily marked and spotted rosy-pink and have a white lip. The flower spikes appear in the spring and take several months to develop, the flowers opening by late summer. It is a good grower in the cool house.

O. longipes

A pretty, dwarf species, 9cm (4in) high, from Brazil. It has small, elongated, usually ribbed pseudobulbs with a single, short, thin leaf. Flower spikes are short, carrying 3–4 flowers, which are quite large for the size of the plant. The petals are chocolate-brown, tipped with yellow, and the lip is yellow. This is a free-flowering species that will take up little room in the cool house, flowering in the summer.

O. luridum

This species is widely distributed throughout the West Indies and parts of the American continent. The pseudobulbs are almost non-existent, the plant mainly

Oncidium cheirophorum is a dwarf species producing masses of small bright yellow, fragrant flowers in the autumn.

consisting of large, leathery leaves, 1–1.2m (3–4ft) long and dark green, sometimes mottled with brown. In its native country, the leaves have given rise to its common name of mule's ear. This plant will produce a quantity of aerial roots. It should be grown in the intermediate or hot house, where it requires maximum sunlight but without scorching, to encourage the flower spikes, which may be anything from 2–3m (6–10ft) long, branched, and bearing many flowers, 3–5cm (1–2in) across, in old gold: they are basically yellow, gently overlaid with blotches of a very light brown.

O. ornithorhynchum

A medium-sized plant, 15cm (6in) high, with oval pseudobulbs and plenty of foliage. It is an extremely free-flowering species for the cool house, often producing three or four spikes per pseudobulb at a time. They are branched and may be arching or pendent. The

Oncidium Sharry Baby 'Sweet Fragrance' is a modern, fragrant, multi-flowered hybrid.

flowers are small, curiously shaped and a very pretty rose-pink with a small, yellow centre. They are strongly fragrant and appear in the autumn or early winter.

O. pulchellum

A dwarf species, 9cm (4in) high, from Jamaica, this orchid bears several short, narrow leaves of a hard texture and is devoid of pseudobulbs. It is usually found on scrubby bushes in almost full sun. The flower spikes can be 45–60cm (18–24in) long, which is extraordinary for such a small plant. The blooms are comparatively large, although very variable, and consist of small sepals and petals which are dominated by the large, rounded lip. The colour may be almost white, suffused with a delicate shade of pink, or a deeper rosy-pink, with a yellow crest. This plant grows in the intermediate house in a position close to the glass.

O. pumilum

This species, 9cm (4in) high, is devoid of pseudobulbs and consists of short, stiff and erect clusters of leaves

resembling the foliage of O. *luridum* but very much smaller. The spikes are upright, 15–20cm (6–8in) tall, dense and branched. The individual blooms are very small, curiously shaped and bright yellow, sometimes spotted with reddish-brown. It flowers at various times of the year and should be grown in the intermediate house.

O. tigrinum

An extremely handsome species that is easy to grow in the cool house, where it is most free-flowering. The plant, which is 15cm (6in) high, has stout pseudobulbs with dark green leaves. The tall flower spikes are sometimes branched and bear large, fragrant flowers with yellow sepals and petals, heavily blotched chocolate-brown. The clear yellow lip is large and spreading. These most attractive blooms will last for many weeks in perfection.

O. triquetrum

Another miniature species, 5cm (2in) high, from Jamaica, the habit resembling that of O. *pulchellum*, but the foliage a little redder. The culture should be the same, in the intermediate house. Short, drooping flower spikes usually carry 4–6 flowers which are white, heavily striped and blotched in brick-red. A free-flowering plant.

O. varicosum

A beautiful plant for the cool house. The oval pseudobulbs grow in clusters, making a plant 15cm (6in) high, and become shrivelled with age; they are usually peppered or spotted with purple-black. The flower spikes are long and arching and may carry many blooms. The most predominant feature of the flowers is the large, bright, intense yellow lip. The small sepals and petals are yellowish-green, marked with brown. This is one of the most popular of the cool-house oncidiums. **var.** *rogersii* is superior to the type.

Hybrids

Most of the hybridizing with oncidiums has been done with other related genera, although there is a selection of *Oncidium* hybrids available. Some intergeneric hybrids containing *Oncidium* are *Odontocidium* (*Odontoglossum* × *Oncidium*) and *Wilsonara* (*Cochlioda* × *Odontoglossum* × *Oncidium*).

OSMOGLOSSUM

Only three very similar species go to make up this tiny genus of pretty epiphytic plants which originate from Mexico and Guatemala. If grown on, they quickly become specimen-sized, when they are seen at their best. They were at one time included with the odontoglossums to which they are closely related, but with which they will not interbreed. No hybrids have been produced.

O. pulchellum (syn. *Odontoglossum pulchellum*)

A very neat and pretty species, 15cm (6in) high, with thin, oblong pseudobulbs, and two narrow leaves. The fragrant flowers are carried on upright spikes, with the lip uppermost. They are small and roundish, waxy-looking, and pure white with bright yellow on the crest of the lip. This little orchid is easy to grow and never fails to flower in the cool house during the spring and summer.

PAPHIOPEDILUM

Paphiopedilums, commonly known as the lady's slipper orchids, number over 60 known species that extend from China across the Himalayas into India and throughout south-east Asia to New Guinea. During the last 20 years of the twentieth century, many new and interesting species were identified from China, Vietnam, Cambodia and Laos, countries previously only partially explored by western botanists.

In the wild they are usually terrestrial but sometimes grow on rocks or occasionally as epiphytes. The plants are bulbless, producing growths of thick, fleshy leaves, these being their reservoir of moisture. The foliage may be plain green or have a beautiful mottled pattern of light and dark green, which makes the plants extremely attractive. Most are of compact size, seldom requiring anything larger than a 10–15cm (4–6in) pot and taking up little room.

The flower spike emerges from the centre of the growth and may carry 1–3 or more flowers. The blooms, which are held upright on the stem, or are sometimes drooping, differ from other orchids in their segments. The top sepal is in most species large, round and very showy. The bottom two sepals are usually insignificant. The lip is formed into a slipper-shaped pouch, hence the common name. The lateral petals are usually large and colourful, and in some species are extremely elongated. The whole impression is of a waxy texture, often shining as if varnished. The main attractions of the paphiopedilums are the longevity of their blooms, which will often last for many months in perfection, and the amazing abundance of colour and design to be found in the petals, which are often lined or covered with hairs and warts.

Being bulbless, these plants should not be allowed to become dry for long periods. They have no definite resting period and should be grown in shady and well-ventilated, cool or intermediate houses. Generally, the plain or green-leaved varieties are cooler-growing than those with mottled foliage. Their shading should be considerable, especially in summer, and strong direct sunlight should be avoided.

A well-drained compost of bark is the most suitable for the hybrids, although a number will flourish in Rockwool. The plants can be propagated readily by carefully removing the back growth as you would remove a back bulb. Cut through the rhizome a few months before the plant is repotted, by which time the severed portion will have started to grow and established itself as a separate plant. A large specimen plant, with several growths, will produce stronger and larger flowers, as well as giving a more pleasing display, so avoid the temptation to chop the plant into single pieces, ending up with small plants that will not flower for some time.

Paphiopedilums remain remarkably free of red spider mite and scale, which readily attack other orchids. The greatest danger lies in overwatering, or allowing water to lie in the top of the growths overnight, especially during periods of low temperature, when decay will quickly set in, resulting in the loss of the growth and possibly the plant.

P. argus

A striking species, originating from the Philippines, this should be grown in the intermediate house and kept well shaded. The foliage is slightly mottled. The plant will flower freely, even off a single growth. It produces a long stem, up to 45cm (18in) tall, carrying a single, large flower. Basically, it is green, the dorsal sepal lightly or heavily striped in purple; the pouch is a dull purple, and the petals striped and spotted with several hairy warts along the top edge. It will last for many

weeks in perfect condition. The flowering period is late spring and early summer.

P. armeniacum

This is a species from China, found growing mainly on outcrops of rock or cliff faces. It is a small, compact plant, 5cm (2in) high, with short, mottled, dark green leaves. It never grows into a large clump, and the flower spike carries a single, large bloom, out of proportion to the plant – a perfect round globe of golden-yellow.

P. bellatulum

A dwarf plant, 5cm (2in) high, from Thailand. The squat foliage is mottled blue-green and covered in a glorious sheen, while the undersides are often rich purple. The leaves are extremely brittle and need care when handling or potting. The flower stem is never more than a few centimetres (inches) long and may bear one, or rarely two, flowers, each approximately 8cm (3in) in diameter. The dorsal sepal and the two petals are large and rounded, giving the flower a cupped appearance, while the pouch is small and egg-shaped. The flower is white, spotted and flushed with reddish-purple. There also exist a few, very rare, albino forms. This orchid is best grown in the intermediate house, where it blooms in late winter or early spring.

P. callosum

An extremely handsome species from Thailand, this orchid is a good and easy grower, often producing several growths at a time, making a plant 10cm (4in) high. The wide leaves are mottled pale green. The tall stem bears a single flower, 10cm (4in) or more across. The large, dominant dorsal is green at the base and heavily lined with purple on a white ground. The slender petals are similarly marked and bear several large black warts on the top edge. The narrow pouch is pale green, sometimes tinted purple. This is one of the coolest-growing of the mottled varieties and is suitable for the warmest end of the cool house, or the intermediate house. Flowering time is spring.

P. concolor

This species is similar in habit and cultural requirements to *P. bellatulum*. The leaves are paler in colour, while the flowers are smaller. The basic colour of the flower is creamy-yellow, with a fine dark peppering.

Paphiopedilum delenatii has large pale pink flowers (above) and attractively mottled foliage (right).

P. delenatii

An extremely handsome species from Vietnam, this plant produces attractively mottled foliage, up to 15cm (6in) wide. The flowers are large, the broad petals white suffused with light pink while the bulbous lip is pink. Until recently a rare plant, it has now been discovered from new localities in China. Grow in the intermediate house.

P. fairieanum

This orchid is a delightful cool-house species that comes from the Himalayas. The foliage is short and pale green, making a plant 10cm (4in) high. The slender stems carry a single, small flower, which is basically green and white. The large dorsal has an extremely wavy edge; purple lines run from its base and become branched at the edges. The petals are drooping, the ends curling upwards; they are outlined with a heavy purple edging and fringed with small hairs. The pouch is narrow and light greeny-brown. Autumn-flowering.

Paphiopedilum Jersey Freckles is a complex hybrid that will flower for several months.

P. hirsutissimum

With long, strap-like, dark green leaves, 12cm (5in) long, this is a robust, cool-house orchid. The flowers are produced on a hairy stem up to 25cm (10in) tall. The comparatively small dorsal is pale-green, heavily peppered with brownish-purple. The long, horizontal petals are club-shaped with extremely wavy edges; the basal half is peppered and spotted with brown, while the tips are pastel pink. The pouch is brown and green. A handsome species, flowering freely in spring.

P. insigne

This orchid has been cultivated since the earliest days of greenhouses, and in the Victorian era there were several dozen named varieties. Unfortunately, few of these are now available. The plant, 12cm (5in) high, consists of plain green leaves and the flower spikes are 20–25cm (8–10in) tall with a single flower produced in winter. The dorsal sepal is green with brown spots and a broad white margin. The petals are brown with green margins and tips. The pouch is similarly coloured and very shiny. The most outstanding variety is **'Harefield Hall'**, which has much larger blooms with a more rounded dorsal. **var.** *sanderae* is greeny-yellow with a green dorsal margined white; the flower is devoid of the brown markings found in the type. These will grow in almost any compost, in the cool end of the cool house.

P. malipoense

A comparatively large, robust plant, 9cm (4in) high, with slightly mottled foliage and a deep purple underside to the leaves. A very tall stem, up to 1m (3ft) high, bears a single, large, apple-green flower with deeper-coloured veined petals, spotting and markings, making it an attractive plant to grow.

P. micranthum

This plant is very similar to *P. armeniacum* but the growth can be larger, 7cm (3in) high, with mottled foliage and stout leaves. The flower is gigantic – up to 12cm (5in) long – with a very large pouch, in a delicate shade of pale pink, dominating the comparatively small, compact petals. The petals are marked with deeper pink, green or yellow patterning. The huge pouch, by far the largest of any of the slipper orchids, explains the common name of bubble gum orchid.

P. niveum

The leaves of this species are similar to *P. bellatulum*, the surface marbled blue-green and the underside purple, but usually a little narrower and shorter. The stem is 10–13cm (4–5in) tall and carries one, or very occasionally two, small flowers, clear of the foliage. They are roundish with a broad dorsal and petals, and a neat pouch. The flower is pure white with a fine peppering of pink near the centre. Pot in a well-drained compost and grow in the intermediate house, or hotter.

P. philippinense

A slow-growing plant, eventually 30cm (12in) high, making large, robust growths with hard, plain green foliage. Spikes, 25cm (10in) long, carry three or four large blooms. The small, white dorsal has a few uneven dark veins, the pouch is ochre-yellow with faint brown lines, and the petals, among the longest of the paphiopedilums, hang down to a length of 12–15cm (5–6in) and are narrow, ribbon-like and twisted throughout their length. The base is green but soon turns to a rich purple for the remaining length. This plant comes from the Philippines and should be grown in the intermediate to hot house. Flowering period is late spring.

P. sanderianum

A handsome, green-leaved species from Borneo, this plant reaches 30cm (12in) high and does best in the intermediate house. It is multi-blooming, the tall spikes carrying up to six large flowers which are overall brownish-purple. The dorsal is pale yellow-green striped, and the extraordinarily long, ribbon-like petals are pale yellow margined with brown-purple. As the flowers open they extend quickly to 60cm (2ft) long. This species, which had not been seen in cultivation for over 100 years and was thought to be extinct, was rediscovered in Borneo growing in vast numbers in a new, previously unexplored habitat. Limited numbers are now being artifically raised from seed and made available to specialist growers.

P. spicerianum

An attractive species, 8cm (3in) high, with dark green leaves, the growths heavily spotted at the base. A single, large bloom is produced. The large, pure white dorsal is dominant. It has a broad, purple streak running from the centre to the tip, while the sides curl backwards. The narrow, pale green petals have wavy edges with a dark line down the centre, while the pouch is greeny-brown. The plant may be accommodated in the cool house, where it will grow alongside *P. insigne*. Autumn-flowering and very long-lasting.

P. sukhakulii

From Thailand, this species has mottled foliage and is very similar to *P. callosum*, being almost indistinguishable when not in flower. Single, large flowers are produced. The small, white dorsal is heavily lined with dark green. The long, flat, smooth-edged petals are held out straight and vary considerably in their colouring, but are usually pale green, densely or lightly spotted with brown-purple. The pouch is pale reddish-green. Suitable for the intermediate house, where its flowers are produced in late summer or autumn.

P. venustum

This species, which reaches 9cm (4in) high, must surely have the most beautiful foliage of all, the leaves being tessellated in deep blue and grey-green, while the undersides are flecked in purple – in some plants completely and evenly coloured. The flowers are modest, particularly for the size of the plant. The dorsal is small and white, heavily lined with green, and the petals are lined with green at the base, are dark pink at the tips and covered in numerous warts and hairs. The orange-yellow pouch is covered in heavy green veins.

Hybrids

Paphiopedilums have been hybridized from the early days of orchid breeding in the late 1800s. Successful

PLATE VIII

Phalaenopsis hybrids

P. Lippeflair

P. Cool Breeze

P. Barbara's Jewel

P. Mivamouche

All flowers are shown at approximately half size

P. Lady Sakara

P. Yellow Treasure

P. Kimberley

P. Ever-spring King

P. Golden Embers

crosses and new hybrids meant that they became very popular. However, they have never been tissue-cultured with the result that each plant, or clone, retains its individuality. Any outstanding plant can only be propagated by the conventional method of dividing when large enough.

The most famous in the multi-flowering group is **P. Saint Swithin**, a hybrid between *P. philippinense* and *P. rothschildianum*. Both these parents are exceedingly slow-growers and when such hybrids are raised from seed, ten years is not unusual before the first plants flower. However, the results are worth waiting for as this is the most spectacular of all orchids. Huge flowers, 3–4 to a stem, have long, pointed petals and a striped and patterned dorsal. They last many months in perfection.

P. Maudiae This, one of the oldest of the mottled-leafed paphiopedilums, is still very popular today. The primary hybrid between *P. callosum* and the albino form of *P. lawrenceanum* has single green and white flowers. The large blooms on an upright stem are com-

Paphiopedilum Sophromore. The downward-sweeping petals give a dramatic stance to this older classic hybrid.

plemented by the beautiful mottled pattern of the foliage, producing a greatly sought-after group of hybrids. An added bonus is their ability to flower from seed after only 3–4 years. This cross has been remade many times and has proved invaluable as a parent.

P. Winston Churchill Raised in the early 1950s, this has proved to be a very important parent, producing some outstanding and award-winning complex types. The very large, almost circular blooms are the result of many years of selected breeding. They are heavily spotted and come in a range of colours from greens and yellows through to the darkest mahogany-browns and reds. One flower is produced at a time, mostly in winter and early spring. They last for weeks in perfection.

PHAIUS

This is a smaller genus than *Calanthe*, but closely related to the evergreen varieties, with the same geographical distribution. The pseudobulbs are small and rounded and usually enclosed by the base of the leaves, which are long and pleated. The flower spike is produced from inside the first leaf and stands erect, well clear of the foliage, carrying a large head of flowers. They are best grown in intermediate house conditions or hotter and, being terrestrial, benefit from a peat-based compost with sand added, which should be kept evenly moist at all times. During the summer months, when the plant is growing fast, watering may be increased accordingly. They are not deciduous, and should be only slightly rested during the winter. Grow in a light, airy position and do not spray with water.

P. tankervilleae (syn. *P. grandifolius*) This is a lovely species, 60cm (2ft) high, with a wide distribution through China, northern India, Burma, Thailand, Malaysia, New Guinea and Australia and the Pacific Islands. A number of geographical varieties occur, causing it to be known under several names. The flower spike will carry up to a dozen or more blooms, each to 10cm (4in) across, not all opening together – usually, the first flower has finished by the time the last flowers open. The backs of the sepals and petals are silvery-white, while the insides are russet-brown with a yellow margin. The trumpet-shaped lip is white and coloured with rosy-purple. The usual flowering period is spring.

PHALAENOPSIS

A large, epiphytic genus noted for its beautiful and extremely long-lasting flowers, which are produced on graceful arching or drooping flower spikes.

The species are found over a wide range extending from India to New Guinea. By far the largest concentration of those in cultivation come from the Philippines and neighbouring islands. The plants always grow in forests where there is plenty of heat and humidity, and are found on the upper branches and trunks of trees. They are typical of monopodials, producing a short, upright stem, with alternate leaves. The foliage is always thick and broad, but the length of the leaf may vary, as also does the colour, which may be dark green or silvery grey-green with mottling. A well-established plant has an extensive root system, mostly aerial. In some species the roots are flat, silver in colour and somewhat wrinkled, readily adhering to anything with which they come into contact.

The flower spike is produced from the axil of the leaf, the racemes being long and branched and bearing many flowers. On a strong plant several spikes may be produced in a year, and a few species may be continuously flowering. Occasionally, new plants will start to grow from the ends of old spikes that have finished flowering. These should be left until they start making their own roots, when they can be removed and potted up separately. The species come in many different colours and are extremely varied. The most commonly cultivated varieties are hybrids in pink, white and yellow, popularly known as moth orchids.

Phalaenopsis are essentially hot-house orchids. The greenhouse should always be shaded, particularly in summer as the foliage is rather tender and will scorch easily. The plants should not be allowed to become dry and during the growing season, when the root system is most active, they should be kept moist. Ventilation should be applied with care, always avoiding a draught.

Repotting these orchids with long, aerial roots, need present no problem. When the compost has deteriorated, rather than disturb active roots, tuck in fresh compost wherever possible. When it is absolutely necessary to repot, prune back the older roots. Several mixtures can be used, but a basic compost of bark or Rockwool is usual. Where a pot deeper than a half-pot is used, half fill with crocks to allow for ample and swift drainage. Phalaenopsis are most rewarding plants to grow, being easy and free-flowering, provided they are given sufficient heat.

P. amabilis

A beautiful species, 22cm (9in) across, with dark green foliage, the leaves thick and broad. The flowering spikes are freely branched and arching with up to 15 or 20 flowers on a stem. They are large, up to 10cm (4in) or more across, and pure white. The lip is white, spotted with red and marked with yellow in the throat. The flowering period varies.

P. equestris

This species has the typical habit and is 15cm (6in) across. The sprays are fairly short, carrying 8–10 small flowers of soft rosy-pink; the lip is spotted. Flowering time is summer.

P. lueddemanniana

There are several named varieties of this species, some incorrectly named as separate species, the variation being so great. The typical plant is 22cm (9in) across, and has broad and long, light green leaves. The flower spikes produce a succession of medium-sized flowers over a period of many months. The sepals and petals are narrow, of equal proportions, basically white to pale yellow, with irregular bars and spots, varying from rosy-pink to dull reddish-brown. The lip is small and narrow and often coloured purple. The plant can be continuous-flowering, producing many spikes which will also easily produce new plantlets.

P. parishii

A dwarf species, seldom more than 12–15cm (5–6in) across, that has short, dark green foliage. Under cultivation, the plant is an evergreen, but in its wild state it becomes deciduous during periods of severe drought. The flower spike is about the same length as the leaf, which is 6cm (2½in) long, and bears miniature, pure white flowers. The loosely hinged lip is comparatively large and broad with two distinct patches of brown. Spring flowering. This species is best grown on a slab of tree fern. It comes from Burma.

P. schilleriana

A handsome plant that grows quite large, with drooping leaves of 60–100cm (24–36in) or more long. They are beautifully patterned with silvery-green markings, often purple on the undersides. The flower spikes can be 78–100cm (31–36in) long, and are profusely branched and drooping. They carry many large and showy flowers, 5–8cm (2–3in) across, which vary from pale pastel-pink to deeper pink, the lateral sepals lightly spotted on the bottom halves. The lip is fiddle-shaped. The flowers open fully, with the tips of the petals curling backwards. Flowering time varies.

P. stuartiana

The foliage of this elegant species is very similar to that of *P. schilleriana*, although not always so heavily marked. The plants are large and robust, 60cm (2ft) across, with long, branching spikes. The flowers are white, the lower halves of the lateral petals spotted with reddish-brown. The lip is also spotted with reddish-purple. Flowering time varies.

Hybrids

In the last twenty years of the twentieth century no other orchid attained such immense popularity as the phalaenopsis. They have become the top houseplant among orchids and are likely to remain so for the foreseeable future. There are more phalaenopsis being hybridized in the world today than any other orchid, such is the massive demand. At one time, the species were considered a novelty and few were grown. Their colour range was limited and their heat demands high, but they have found a niche in modern centrally heated homes. They flower more quickly from seed than almost any other orchid: fully mature plants of blooming size are raised within three years. With selected breeding and improved techniques that time will be reduced even further. Once in flower, they last for a very long time, thriving in the dry atmosphere of the home where the blooms remain in perfection without spoiling or damping off. Fewer phalaenopsis are grown by serious amateurs and the majority are for the windowsill culture.

Some commercial growers are no longer concerned with names of breeding lines as each year many thousands of crosses are being raised and remain unregistered. Improved laboratory techniques mean that the very best of the new hybrids can be reselected and tissue-cultured, resulting in the rarest colours becoming available.

P. Cool Breeze is an example of the ever-popular large, round, white-flowered type of phalaenopsis. The flowers, with yellow lips, are produced on long arching sprays. It comes from a long line of hybrids which can be traced back to the Philippino species *P. amabilis*, which has had the most influence on the size, shape and long-lasting qualities.

P. Golden Bells gives fine, pale yellow flowers on shorter spikes and was raised from such species as *P. lueddemanniana* from the Philippines. The smaller-flowered yellow species were never considered of such importance as the larger-flowered whites until they were hybridized, resulting in a whole new group of highly desirable plants.

P. Lipperose is typical of large, modern pink varieties that can be traced back to the species *P. schilleriana* and *P. sanderiana*, which have dominated all hybrids with this colouring. When *P. amabilis* is included in the breeding line, the size and shape is improved. *P. Lipperose* has been much used as a parent to produce even better and darker pinks which are readily available today.

PHRAGMIPEDIUM

This remarkable genus, consisting of a few species, was very popular with Victorian growers and there were several notable collections of just phragmipediums, in those days known as selenepediums.

Phragmipedium species come from tropical America where they grow as terrestrials or sometimes on rocks. They are best with the warm house paphiopedilums and their culture is the same, although, since they make larger plants with taller spikes, they will need more room.

They nearly all produce long, strap-like, pale to dark green foliage, with tall spikes each bearing 3–4 flowers or more, depending upon the species. In some the flowers open in succession. The predominant colours are green-buff to pink. The pouch is often large and the dorsal sepal narrow, pointed and drooping. The lateral petals can be very narrow and ribbon-like. It is fascinating to watch these flowers open. The petals are the same length as the other portions of the bloom, and quickly start to grow, spiralling downwards until they attain their full length.

Phragmipedium Don Wimber. Sequential flowering will keep this orchid in bloom for months.

P. besseae

This delightful species is unique among the genus for its brilliant red colouring. Discovered as recently as 1981, it comes from Peru and Ecuador, where it grows in inaccessible places, mainly on vertical rock faces. It grows to 15cm (6in) across, and produces glossy green leaves along a creeping rhizome. One to four large flowers are borne on an upright stem, 45cm (18in) high. The petals are short and rounded, the pouch orange-red and small.

P. caudatum

A well-known species from Central and South America. The plants are strong and robust and 30cm (12in) high. The flower spikes are tall and bear 1–4 flowers. Large and spectacular, these are lightly coloured buff-brown and have extremely long and thin petals which grow rapidly once the flower is open.

P. longifolium

This species is 1m (3ft) high and has long, narrow leaves of dark glossy green. The large flowers open in succession over a long period as the spike extends to 1.5m (5ft). Individually they are pale-coloured, green

Pleione speciosa is a small, spring-flowering species with comparatively large blooms.

and light pink on the rigidly held petals, which extend to just below the pouch. The plants bloom mainly during the summer and originate from Central and South America.

P. pearcei

A smaller species, 22cm (9in) high, with thin, grasslike foliage on tufted growths. The neat flowers are greenish with rigidly-held petals.

P. sargentianum

A tall, robust plant, 1m (3ft) high, which blooms over many months, producing a succession of large blooms on a spike 1.5m (5ft) long. These are delicately coloured in light green with some purple on the petals. The petals are long and ribbon-like, twisted in their length and held stiffly out from the flower. Originally introduced from Brazil.

Hybrids

Among the species, *P. caudatum* and *P. longifolium* have produced several good hybrids. The best of these is **P. Grande**, which was first recorded in 1881, when it was considered to be of exceptional merit and, indeed, this is still true today. It is easily the most robust and the best to grow, producing large, beautiful blooms.

With the discovery of *P. besseae*, hybridizing took off afresh, and with the better understanding of genetics, plants from the previous century were resurrected and crossed with the new species to produce fantastic pinks and reds, and all the shades between. This has given a new concept to the genus.

P. China Dragon (*P. Grande* × *P. besseae*) One of the largest of the *Phragmipedium* hybrids, producing pale pink flowers up to the size of *P. Grande*.

P. Eric Young (*P. besseae* × *P. longifolium*) One of the finest *Phragmipedium* hybrids ever, this produces salmon-pink flowers on tall spikes. When the first flower drops off, a new one comes in a few weeks.

P. Memoria Dick Clements (*P. sargentianum* × *P. besseae*) Tall spikes with very dark red flowers in succession.

PLEIONE

Pleiones are extremely popular and easy to grow, often being placed alongside alpine plants in gardens or alpine house. They are found at high altitudes, often on the snow line in the Himalayas as far as China and across to the island of Taiwan. The plants consist of squat, round pseudobulbs of annual duration, each with a single, deciduous leaf. In the spring, when the new growth develops, the flower spike is produced from the centre. It usually has one bloom which is large for the size of the pseudobulb, being 8–10cm (3–4in) across, and lasts a week to 10 days. The sepals and petals are equal in size, usually delicate pink and the lip is large, frilled and spotted.

The plants should be repotted annually, either before or just after flowering, but certainly before new roots appear. Any number of bulbs may be potted together to fill a large pan. During the summer months give copious supplies of water and a liquid feed. As the new pseudobulb matures, the old one decays completely. An individual pseudobulb will often produce two growths from the base, and also numerous terminal bulblets from the top of the pseudobulb, which will quickly grow on to flowering size.

When the season's growth has been completed, the foliage is discarded by the plant as activity ceases. All that is necessary during the winter is to keep the bulbs away from frost; they need no attention at all.

P. formosana

This is the most popular of all the pleiones. Its pseudobulbs are dark green or purple, making a plant 15cm (6in) high, and the flowers are soft delicate pink with a large, frilly lip which is variable, but usually creamy-white with numerous brown spots and a yellow throat. It is easily propagated, and flowers in the spring.

P. humilis

This species is 9cm (4in) high. The pseudobulbs are small, pear-shaped and dark green to purple. At 5cm (2in) across, the flowers are smaller than in *P. formosana*, with white sepals and petals, sometimes faintly

Pleione Versailles 'Muriel Turner' is a sturdy hybrid that blooms in the spring.

spotted purple. The lip is white with reddish-brown markings. It blooms during the winter.

P. praecox

The pseudobulbs of this species are squarish, with a depression around the apex, and dark green, heavily spotted with purple-brown. The plant is 15cm (6in) high. The large flowers are produced in the autumn or early winter and are rich rosy-purple, the lip usually darker. This species grows more in the winter, and it is, therefore, advisable to keep it at a slightly higher temperature than the two previous species.

P. speciosa

A small-growing *Pleione*, 10cm (4in) high when in leaf. It blooms in the spring producing a single, brightly coloured flower, which is large for the size of the plant. The petals and sepals are rich cerise and the lip is similarly coloured. Grow very cool and give a frost-free environment during the winter.

Hybrids

Hybridization has increased the range of colours, mainly different shades of pink and purple, with some yellow and white. **P. Shantung** is rich yellow and orange with a large, frilly, patterned lip.

PLEUROTHALLIS

Almost 1,000 individual species constitute this genus, making it the largest group of orchids to be found in tropical America. The variation among the species is very wide, in both foliage and blooms, but nearly all of them make miniature plants resembling the masdevallias – to which they are closely allied – in habit. The single leaves are usually carried on a slender stem, slightly longer than the leaf, from the top of which come the flowers. The sepals are normally the most dominant feature, while the petals and lip are more often less conspicuous. Colours vary greatly, often being translucent. The flowers, which are usually very small, may be in ones or twos or there may be a great profusion in long sprays in some species. While a number of the species are very showy, by far the greater proportion are of botanical interest only. However, as they take up such little room in small pans hung close to the glass, they have a novelty interest, growing and flowering freely. They require the same cultural conditions in the cool house as masdevallias.

P. ghiesbrechtiana

This variable species has leaves of medium height at 10cm (4in), with brown sheathing at the base. The spikes, which are taller than the foliage at up to 22cm (9in) long, are many-flowered. The attractive blooms are set close to the stem.They are small, orange and long-lasting. Comes mainly from Mexico and flowers in the spring.

P. minutiflora

This has leaves that are very small, thick and rounded, dark green and speckled on the undersides. Flower spikes are erect, 5cm (2in) long, extremely thin, carrying up to six minute blooms which are translucent white, with little marking.

P. pachyglossa

Large, roundish foliage carried on tall stems. The spikes are produced from the base of the leaf with several translucent pink or dull purple flowers that appear late summer; its origin is Mexico.

P. tribuloides

A plant about 5cm (2in) high; the supporting stem is very short and the flowers are produced low down, nestling among the foliage. Numerous blooms of a brick-red colour are produced in the late spring.

PROMENAEA

This genus consists of a small number of epiphytic species, all of which come from Brazil and are well worth growing. The plants are closely allied to zygopetalums, and are dwarf in habit, bearing small pseudobulbs and several leaves. The attractive flowers, usually solitary, are large for the size of the plant, with sepals and petals of equal size. They are best planted in a fine bark compost in small pans in the intermediate house and should be kept growing continuously. A fairly sunny position close to the glass will suit them. When repotting, all old compost should be removed, to avoid any souring.

P. stapelioides

This species has short, bluey-green foliage borne on rounded pseudobulbs which grow in clusters and readily make two or more growths at a time. The flowers are pale yellow, the sepals and petals heavily spotted with reddish-purple. Neither this nor *P. xanthina* is more than 8cm (3in) high, even when in flower. Flowering period varies.

P. xanthina

This is a very popular species, with a habit the same as *P. stapelioides*; the plants are indistinguishable when not in flower. The flowers are about 5cm (2in) across, clear citron-yellow, the lip heavily spotted with red on the sides and base. The long-lasting blooms appear at various times of the year. The habit of making two or more growths make this a very easily propagated plant.

Hybrids

Promenaea hybridizing has only recently began to make an impact. The species have much to offer in intergeneric crossings with other related genera. Their attractive colourings and markings can add significantly to those of zygopetalums, for example. Among the most striking of the intergeneric hybrids are *Alangreatwoodara* (*Zygopetalum* × *Colax* × *Promenaea*). Plants are now being produced which combine some fragrance with attractive blooms on short flower spikes, often two or more to a growth.

PSYCHOPSIS (SYN. ONCIDIUM)

This is a small genus of delightful and fanciful species from Central and South America and the West Indies, known as the butterfly orchids. Until recently they were included in the genus *Oncidium*, but are now separated into their own genus. They can be in bloom at any time of the year and are epiphytes that can be grown in pots or mounted on bark slabs.

P. krameriana

The pseudobulbs of this species are tightly clustered, flat and often wrinkled. They are dark purplish-brown, bearing a single leaf of similar colour and hard, leathery texture. The plant is 20cm (8in) high. The flowering spike is 1–1.2m (3–4ft) long and bears one single, large bloom at a time. This lasts up to two weeks and is followed by another within a few more weeks. This succession of blooming from the end of the flower spike may last for many months, and even years. The extraordinary flower has a dorsal sepal and two petals of about 7cm (3in) long and held erect, while the lateral petals and lip are frilly. The whole flower is yellow, spotted and blotched with chestnut markings. They are plants for the hot house.

P. papilio

The companion to *P. krameriana*. The flowers vary only slightly and are larger, with a flattened upper sepal. The lateral petals are longer and less frilly. They are heavily marked with reddish-brown on a yellow ground. Both these plants require a rest during the winter, and usu-

ally prefer to be kept on the dry side for the remainder of the year, needing a fairly light position in the hot house.

PSYGMORCHIS (SYN. ONCIDIUM)

This is a small genus containing less than six delightful, dwarf species, related to the oncidiums, and at one time included in that genus because of the similarities between their flowers. The plants are epiphytic and come from South and Central America.

P. pusilla

One of the prettiest orchids to grow, this miniature has no pseudobulbs and the foliage is arranged in a perfectly flat, fan-like formation, making a plant no more than 5–8cm (2–3in) high. The new leaves are continually produced from the centre of the plant. The flower spikes appear, several at a time, from in between the axils of the leaves. They usually bear a succession of large, single, yellow flowers, of which the lip is the main feature. The base of the petals and the crest of the lip are delicately peppered with red. The plant grows best in a shady position in the intermediate house, where it should not be allowed to remain dry for long periods.

RENANTHERA

This is a small genus of epiphytic orchids that produce slender stems with a row of leaves on each side. One or two of the species attain great heights in their natural habitat. Their growth and cultivation resembles that of vandas. Although widely distributed throughout south-east Asia and the Philippines, only one or two are seen in collections today.

R. imschootiana

The plant does not grow excessively tall, reaching 30cm (12in) high. The long flower spikes are branching and carry many long-lasting flowers, the individual blooms being quite large. The petals and upper sepals are short and narrow, while the two lateral sepals are narrow at the base broadening out until they become very large and rounded. The lip is very small and insignificant. The top half of the bloom is orange-red, the petals blotched and spotted, while the two large sepals are more richly coloured. The plant blooms freely in the spring. Grow in the intermediate house.

Hybrids

Much intergeneric breeding has been achieved using the red-flowered species to give colour and variability to other related genera. Renantheras will cross with *Rhynchostylis* to give *Renanstylis*, with *Vanda* to give *Renantanda*, and *Phalaenopsis* to give *Renanthopsis*. These, and many others, are tropical orchids, raised and grown mainly in warm climates.

RHYNCHOSTYLIS

At the present time only four epiphytic species form this very small genus. The plants are of typical monopodial habit, producing short stems. They are noted mostly for the density of their flower spikes, which are usually produced freely when the plant is grown alongside intermediate-house vandas. Although only a small genus they are widely distributed throughout India, Indonesia, Malaysia and the Philippines.

R. retusa

This species, which grows to 30cm (12in) high, produces long, pendent, cylindrical racemes up to 30cm (12in) long, containing many small flowers densely packed on the spike to give it its common name of fox tail orchid. The individual blooms are white, the segments spotted with pink, while the small lip is magenta-purple. The flowering period is spring. This is a showy orchid and easy to grow.

Hybrids

This genus has been used considerably to produce intergeneric hybrids such as *Rhynchanthera* (*Renanthera* × *Rhynchostylis*), *Rhynchopsis* (*Phalaenopsis* × *Rhynchostylis*) and *Rhynchovanda* (*Rhynchostylis* × *Vanda*). These orchids need year-round sunshine to grow and flower well, so are mainly seen in the tropical parts of the world.

RODRIGUEZIA

A comparatively small genus of epiphytic orchids from Brazil and other parts of South America, where they inhabit the tropical regions. The plants have rather small, flattened pseudobulbs, which produce several stiff, dark green leaves. The short, arching flower spikes arise from the base, and flower profusely. The sepals and petals are of equal proportions, while the lip is large and the whole flower has a crystalline texture.

These are plants that like their roots to be in the air and, therefore, do well when attached to pieces of wood and placed in a shady position in the intermediate house. Otherwise, grow in small pans, where the compost should be kept sweet. Water should be given throughout the year, the plants resting only slightly during the winter.

R. secunda

A very pretty species, 15cm (6in) tall, with an arching spike up to 15cm (6in) long. The flowers are arranged in two rows on top of the spike and are rosy-pink. Summer-flowering or at various times.

R. venusta

A charming species, 15cm (6in) high, with pendent spikes of highly fragrant, pure white flowers, which have a large spreading lip, stained with yellow.

ROSSIOGLOSSUM (SYN. ODONTOGLOSSUM)

This is a small genus of about six species from Central America which were at one time included in the genus *Odontoglossum*. (Plants can still be found under that earlier name.) They are robust orchids, producing stout pseudobulbs, each with a pair of wide, dark green leaves. They need a decided rest in the winter while they are not growing and are often slow to commence their growth in the spring. The flower spikes arise during the summer from the base of the partly mature pseudobulbs. The large, flamboyant and glossy blooms appear during the autumn and last for up to three weeks. Grow the plants in the cool house with good light in winter.

R. grande

This large-flowered and showy species is easily grown in the cool house, where it needs a decided rest with full light during the winter. It has stout, bluish-green pseudobulbs with thick, leathery, dark green leaves, making a plant 20cm (8in) high. The flower spike appears in the autumn and carries 3–5 large flowers. The sepals and petals are rich glossy yellow, banded and blotched with bright chestnut-brown. The small, roundish lip is creamy-white and marked with reddish-brown. Its common name of clown orchid is due to the man-like formation in the centre of the flower. It comes from Guatemala.

R. schlieperianum

This plant resembles *R. grande* – the flowers are similar but there are more of them per upright spike and they are mostly pale yellow, banded with reddish-brown. A native of Costa Rica, it flowers in the autumn and requires the same treatment as *R. grande*.

Hybrids

Only one hybrid, **R. Jawdon Jester** (*R. grande* × *R. williamsianum*) has been produced. The flowers are large and colourful and the plant is more easily obtainable than the species.

SOPHRONITIS

A genus of miniature orchids that come from Brazil, where they grow on mossy trees and rocks. There are several delightful species with large, red-coloured flowers, which are well worth growing. The plants make very small pseudobulbs that each carry a single, thick leaf. All do well in the cool house, where they occupy very little room: when in bloom, they are seldom more than 5–8cm (2–3in) high. Grow these plants in shallow pans or half-pots in fine bark in a shady position where they can be kept evenly moist throughout the year. When grown on into specimen plants, they are a beautiful sight.

S. cernua

The pseudobulbs of this orchid are very fat with round, thick, grey-green leaves. They produce 1–4 small flowers; the sepals and petals are a cinnabar-red and the lip is the same colour with an orange throat. Flowering period is winter, when they will last a long time in perfection.

S. coccinea

Easily the most charming and best-known of the genus, this species produces blooms that are perfectly flat and bright scarlet-red with an orange-yellow throat. The long-lasting flowers,which are produced in the spring, are often 5cm (2in) across, sometimes as much as 8cm (3in) on a well-grown plant.

S. rosea

Pseudobulbs squat with rounded, blue-green leaves. The blooms are rich rose-pink with a tint of purple, and extremely pretty.

S. violacea (syn. *Sophronitella violacea*)

A more slender plant, with pseudobulbs growing close together. The flowers may sometimes appear in twos, but more usually are single. They are a variable dark-violet.

Hybrids

This miniature genus has played an important part in hybridization. *S. coccinea* has been crossed with laelias, cattleyas and other relatives through the ages, and has much to offer this line of breeding. It is the jewel in the crown of intergeneric *Cattleya* hybridizing, and has helped to miniaturize this otherwise large-flowered group.

Sophrolaeliocattleya Hazel Boyd One of the most outstanding of the *Sophronitis* hybrids, having all the fine characteristics of the small, compact-growing plant but with large flowers. Most of them are golden-yellow or apricot with some red markings. It is a hybrid from *Sophrolaeliocattleya* Jewel Box, already mentioned under *Cattleya*; the *Sophronitis* is really famous for this type of miniature breeding.

STANHOPEA

This genus includes species with the most incredible flowers. They are distributed throughout tropical America, where they are epiphytic, growing on trees in similar habitats to the gongoras. The flower spike is produced from the base of the pseudobulb and penetrates the compost to emerge underneath the plant, where it will bear a small number of very large, highly fragrant flowers. The buds develop quickly and the flowers can pop open suddenly, usually early in the morning. The petals are thrown back, exposing the large, broad column and the extraordinary lip, which together are a heavy waxy texture. Their beautiful fragrance will fill the greenhouse, but sadly this perfection lasts only two or three days.

The following species are all good for the intermediate house, where they grow in a well-drained compost in slatted baskets, so that the flower spikes can easily emerge through the bottom or sides. Water the plants carefully at all times, bearing in mind that plants potted in this manner tend to dry out more quickly. During the period of flowering, watering should be withheld so as to avoid wetting the flower spike.

Stanhopea grandiflora produces highly fragrant though short-lived flowers. It is best cultivated in a basket.

S. eburnea

This species produces 1–2-flowered spikes with large, ivory-white blooms with a fine peppering of purple. It is strongly lemon-scented. The flowering period is early summer. It comes from Trinidad and Brazil and makes a plant 45cm (18in) high.

S. grandiflora

This South American, summer-flowering species is very effective in a basket, where it will grow to 30cm (12in) high. The pendent flower spikes produce ivory white, waxy, highly scented blooms that last for a few days only.

S. tigrina

The most striking and popular of the stanhopeas, this species reaches 45cm (18in) high and has 2–4-flowered spikes. The blooms are very large but somewhat variable in colour, the typical form being yellow, the sepals and petals lightly or heavily blotched with maroon,

while the base of the lip, the column and the remainder are spotted dull purple. A native of Mexico, this species flowers during the summer.

S. wardii

Bearing up to 7–8 flowers, sometimes more, this species has smaller blooms that vary from yellow to orange, the petals and sepals lightly spotted reddish-brown. The lip is paler with a large, dark blotch at the base. Flowering time is late summer to autumn.

THUNIA

This is a very small, but attractive genus, the species all from Burma. They are terrestrial and produce tall, thin, reed-like stems up to 1m (3ft) long with beautiful pale green, soft-textured foliage. The leaves are arranged alternately along the whole length of the stem-like pseudobulb. A large drooping head of blooms arises from the apex in the summer.

In the spring, when the new growth appears, pot up in a rich compost of peat and sand, keep dry until the new growth is several centimetres (inches) high. Take care not to get the young leaves wet or they may quickly damp off. Once a root system has commenced, and the plant is growing fast, give liberal amounts of water and fertilizer. The plant can remain in a moist condition until the autumn, when the leaves will turn yellow and be shed from the newly completed pseudobulb, the old one having shrivelled and become exhausted. During the winter, the dry stems can be stored in full light in a cool and dry position until the new growth is seen.

Propagation is easily achieved by removing the old pseudobulb when the new one is half-completed, cutting this into sections in between the nodes, and placing these in a propagating frame. Grow in either the cool or intermediate house, where a fairly light and airy position suits them. The foliage should be kept dry.

T. marshalliana

This easily-grown species blooms profusely with large flower heads carrying a succession of up to 12 short-lived flowers, the racemes lasting for perhaps a month. The delicately textured sepals and petals are white and of equal proportions. The lip is trumpet-shaped and deeply fringed, with an orange or yellow throat. An attractive summer-flowering plant.

TRICHOPILIA

There are about 30 known species of these showy epiphytic orchids, widely distributed throughout the Americas. The pseudobulbs are neat and flattened, and carry a solitary leaf. The blooms are produced from the base of the pseudobulb. The orchids grow at high elevations and, therefore, do best in the cool house or at the coolest end of the intermediate house. After the season's growth has been completed, the plants should be slightly rested, keeping the atmosphere around them on the dry side, as the foliage may spot easily.

T. tortilis

A pretty species, 15cm (6in) high, with pendent spikes, each bearing a single bloom; several spikes may be produced at a time. The fragrant, long-lasting flowers are large and up to 15cm (6in) across, the sepals and petals equal, narrow and twisted lengthways. They are pale pink, greeny-yellow at the edges. The lip is broad, trumpet-shaped at the base and spreading. It is white, spotted with pale brown. This plant is a native of Mexico and Honduras.

VANDA

This large genus contains about 70 species and is among the most gorgeous and popular of all orchids, being grown widely around the world. The species originate from a wide area bounded by China in the north and North Australia in the south; they are found from Sri Lanka to many of the Pacific islands. Nearly always epiphytic and sometimes lithophytic, vandas are found wherever there is an abundance of moisture and humidity. They are monopodial, producing a single stem and growing continuously from the top. The leaves are formed in two rows down each side of the stem. These leaves divide the vandas into two groups. In the smaller group, the leaves are cylindrical. Those in the larger group produce a strap-like leaf with a deep ridge down the middle; the ends are usually blunt, giving the appearance of being broken.

The root system, which is usually fairly extensive, is produced from the bottom half of the stem. During the main periods of growth activity, their bright green tips are followed by a white, papery covering – the velamen. Many of the roots prefer to remain in the air, rather than enter the compost. They grow to considerable lengths in some plants, and become branched, as in the phalaenopsis, adhering to anything with which they come into contact.

The flower spikes appear from the axils of the leaves, on the upper parts of the plant, but never from the centre. Some of these spikes may be very long, bearing many flowers. Nearly all the species are showy and well worth growing; one or two are strongly scented. As may be expected from a group of plants with such a wide geographical distribution, their flowers have considerable variations in colour and size. Yellow, green and brown are represented, some heavily spotted; there is also blue, a rare colour in orchids. In most species the petals rotate completely at the base shortly after the flower opens; they carry on twisting until the outside is facing inwards.

Among the species, there are plants that grow in both the cool and intermediate sections. Vandas should not be allowed to become completely dry, and watering may be done frequently, with more attention when the roots are most active. The long aerial roots may be sprayed daily, adding a liquid feed during the summer months. While a number of the species are free-flowering, it is essential to give most of them an abundance of light for flowers to be obtained. Many of the shorter-growing varieties will do best in a sunny position suspended from the rafters close to the glass. Fresh air is beneficial to these plants and should be given whenever possible, at the same time avoiding any direct draught. The intermediate varieties will do well when grown alongside cattleyas. These plants rest only slightly during the winter, if at all, and this is indicated by the covering up of the growing root-tips. During this period, watering should be gradually reduced, but not withheld altogether.

As these orchids shed their lower leaves, they become tall and 'leggy'. Provided the plant has made sufficient roots high enough up the stem, it may be cut through to reduce the height. Where no such roots have been made, encourage them by wrapping the stem in a polythene sleeve packed with wet sphagnum moss. Within a few months, new roots should have appeared, and the plant may be cut down. The remaining stump will sometimes start to grow again. This is a valuable way of increasing these plants, which are not readily propagated. Occasionally, side growths will be produced from an ordinary plant which, when they have their own root system, may be removed.

PLATE IX

Phragmipedium hybrids and *Paphiopedilum* hybrids

Phragmipedium Sorcerer's Apprentice

Phragmipedium Longueville

Paphiopedilum Helvetia 'Burnham'

All flowers are shown at approximately half size

Phragmipedium Mont Fallu

Phragmipedium
Saint Peter

Paphiopedilum Delophyllum

Paphiopedilum Helvetia

V. amesiana

The orchid has short stems 15cm (6in) high, with semi-cylindrical leaves that have a groove on the surface. Erect, sometimes branched spikes bear 10–15 flowers, which are small and white, tinted with rose; the small lip is of a darker shade. Usually fragrant; flowers in the early part of the year.

V. coerulea

A high-elevation species from the Himalayas and particularly Burma, suitable for the cool house. The plants can grow to 1m (3ft) tall; the leaves are stiff and held horizontally, and may be up to 25cm (10in) long. The flower spikes bloom in the autumn, carrying up to a dozen flowers. These are highly variable, from white with merely a tint of blue to a clear sky-blue; good blue varieties are rare. The colour usually appears as a mottling on the sepals and petals. The small lip is usually much darker. The size and colour of the blooms usually improve within a day or two of their opening.

V. coerulescens

This plant resembles V. coerulea in habit, but the flower spikes are shorter, and the smaller blooms are a darker, more purplish-blue, with a rich violet lip, also highly variable. This plant does better at a slightly higher temperature than V. coerulea, preferably at the coolest end of the intermediate house.

V. cristata (syn. Trudelia cristata)

This charming miniature forms a short, compact plant seldom more than 25cm (10in) high. During the early summer 2–3 spikes may be produced, each with 1–2 blooms. These are greeny-yellow with a white lip marked with deep maroon lines. An easy plant to grow and flower in the cool house.

V. sanderiana (syn. Euanthe sanderiana)

This species must surely rank supreme among the vandas, although it is now mostly labelled as Euanthe, a genus created solely for it; the older name of Vanda is retained for registration of hybrids. The plant, 45cm (18in) high, is typical of vandas in habit. The rounded flowers, up to 12cm (5in) across, are flat and strikingly marked. The upper sepal and petals are white with a tinge of pink, and spotted at the base. The two lower sepals are a little larger and yellow, heavily veined red away from the centre. The small, fleshy lip is orangey-yellow. A native of the Philippines, it is best grown in the hot house.

V. teres

This plant is capable of growing to great heights, but under cultivation seldom exceeds 1m (3ft). The stem is hard and woody with cylindrical leaves spaced at intervals of several centimetres (inches). The spikes bear 4–5 blooms, 8–10cm (3–4in) across. The sepals are white, tinged with rose, while the petals are larger, more rounded and of a much deeper colour. The lip is large, much darker, and usually spotted in the throat. To induce this plant to flower, give maximum light at all times and rest during the winter, which is contrary to general Vanda culture. The intermediate house will suit it.

V. tricolor

A robust plant, up to 2m (6ft) high, with long, strap-like leaves. The spikes are short, with up to six flowers, each 7cm (3in) across. Sepals and petals are about the same size and are pale yellow, heavily spotted with reddish-brown. The petals twist after the flower has been open for a few days. The lip is purple. This plant, which is quite capable of flowering twice in one year, is a native of Java and should be grown in the hot house.

Hybrids

In the genus Vanda, a great amount of hybridizing has been done, but more so in hotter countries: because these plants thrive and flower freely in almost full sunlight, they are not ideal subjects for cooler climates. Most hybridizing has been done in Florida, Singapore, Taiwan and Thailand. The blue V. coerulea played a dominant part with the primary crosses, and is still doing so. One of the most famous hybrids it produced is V. Rothschildiana, a cross with V. sanderiana (Euanthe sanderiana), itself an important parent. In V. Rothschildiana can be seen the perfect shape of the one, combined with the beautiful blue of the other.

It is possible to interbreed the cylindrical-leaved vandas with the strap-leaved plants, a famous example being V. Nellie Morley, which is a combination of V. teres, V. tricolor and V. sanderiana.

Interbreeding is possible with nearly all the allied genera, and as interest spreads in this field, more surprising crosses are being produced all the time. As taxonomists take a second look at many of the species, they find it necessary to reclassify many of them, placing them among different genera, and sometimes even creating a new genus to accommodate them. This has caused considerable confusion for the hybrid registrar, as many of the parents recorded are still being registered under their old botanical names.

ZYGOPETALUM

This is a comparatively small genus, the majority of the species coming from Brazil. They have a terrestrial habit, produce round pseudobulbs with plenty of foliage, and the spikes are produced from inside the first or second leaf when the growth is half completed. The long-lasting, often strongly scented flowers are carried on tall spikes. These plants do well when cultivated under similar conditions to cymbidiums in the cool house, although a slightly higher temperature during the winter is beneficial. Grow them in a well-drained compost which may have the addition of peat.

Z. crinitum

This species produces plants 22cm (9in) tall, that bear highly fragrant blooms during the spring. The large flowers have narrow sepals and petals that are brownish, while the large lip is white, streaked with violet-mauve.

Z. intermedium (syn. *Z. mackaii*)

This is a very popular orchid with its tall, handsome spikes of many flowers, each 7cm (3in) across. The equal-sized sepals and petals are green, blotched and spotted with brown, while the large, rounded lip is white, heavily streaked with purple. Flowers are produced during autumn and winter.

Zygopetalum Perrenoudi is one of the first hybrids, bringing out darker colouring and fragrance.

Hybrids

Zygopetalum hybrids are starting to make an impact, particularly where intergeneric crosses are being produced. Some striking results are being obtained with *Zygoneria (Neogardneria × Zygopetalum)* and *Zygocolax (Colax × Zygopetalum)* among others. Small plants that produce an abundance of fragrant blooms in greens and browns are proving ideal for the hobbyist.

APPENDICES

Adventitious New growth or roots coming from a node on the stem.

Back bulb The older leafless pseudobulbs situated at the back of a sympodial orchid.

Bifoliate A plant that produces two leaves on each pseudobulb, mostly used in reference to cattleyas.

Bigeneric hybrid A hybrid between two separate genera.

Bract A leafy membrane protecting young growth or buds.

Column A finger-like structure at the centre of the orchid flower that contains pollen and the stigmatic patch.

Epiphyte An orchid that grows on a tree but takes nothing from it, i.e. an air plant.

Flower spike The stem that carries the flowers. It may come from the base of the plant or the apex of the pseudobulb.

Front division The part of an orchid that is leafy and has the younger growth.

Hirsute Any part of a plant that is covered with hairs.

Intergeneric hybrid A hybrid that possesses more than two separate genera in its make-up.

Labellum (lip) The third petal on an orchid flower that has evolved into a landing platform for the pollinating insect.

Lithophyte An orchid that grows upon rocks, rather like an epiphyte.

Meristem culture A method of mass-propagation by culturing tissue cells taken from one plant.

Monopodial An orchid that produces an upward-growing rhizome from which grow pairs of leaves.

Mycorrhiza A fungus that forms an association with orchid seed to enable both to co-exist.

Node The part of the stem where flowers or new growth will emerge.

Pollen cap (anther) A protective cap that covers the pollen masses found at the end of the column.

Pollinia The pollen masses of the orchid flower, which consist of solid packs of pollen grains.

Primary hybrid A hybrid with two species as its parents.

Protocorm An embryo that forms from the seed before leaves and roots can be produced.

Pseudobulb A swollen stem at the base of sympodial orchids, this holds the water reserves for the plant.

Rhizome The woody stem by which pseudobulbs or growths are joined.

Roots Orchids produce seasonal roots that die naturally as the leaves are shed. Aerial roots are exposed to the air.

Sepals The three segments that form the outer whorl of an orchid flower, in orchids similar to the petals. The dorsal sepal is at the top of the flower. The two lateral sepals are lower and on either side.

Stigmatic patch A sticky depression found on the underside of the column, where pollen is deposited.

Symbiotic The relationship between an orchid seed and its mycorrhizal fungus which aids fertilization.

Sympodial An orchid that produces independent seasonal growth from the previous year's growth.

Terete Foliage that is rounded, like a pencil.

Terrestrial An orchid that grows in the ground.

Unifoliate An orchid that carries a single leaf on a pseudobulb, mostly used in reference to cattleyas.

Velamen An absorbent, white, outer covering of a root, the velamen soaks up water and nutrients from the surroundings.

Odontioda Victoria Village is a modern white hybrid, bred from the species *Odontoglossum crispum*.

APPENDIX 2
ABOUT THE AUTHORS

Brian Rittershausen is Managing Director of Burnham Nurseries Ltd.

Wilma Rittershausen is a freelance writer and the editor of *The Orchid Review*, orchid journal of the Royal Horticultural Society.

Sara Rittershausen is the third generation of the same family to run Burnham Nurseries Ltd.

In 1953 Percy Rittershausen, founder of Burnham Nurseries Ltd, wrote the highly acclaimed *Successful Orchid Culture*. This was the first new orchid book to appear on the market for 20 years and was selected by the British Book League as one of the 100 best books of the year. Since that time there has never been a period when a Rittershausen orchid book has not been available. Continuous demand for our books has kept us writing.

The American Orchid Society has called us 'The UK's most prolific writers of orchid books'. Our books are in demand the world over and a number have been translated into several other languages, while special editions have been issued for the USA.

APPENDIX 3
READING ABOUT ORCHIDS

Orchids: A Hamlyn Care Manual
Brian and Sara Rittershausen
Hamlyn 2000

Orchids: The New Plant Library
Consultant Brian Rittershausen
Lorenz Books 1999

Orchids The Royal Horticultural Society
Brian and Wilma Rittershausen
Quadrille 1999

Orchids – Their Care and Cultivation
Brian and Wilma Rittershausen
Antique Collectors Club Ltd 2001

Practical Encyclopaedia of Orchids
Brian and Wilma Rittershausen
Lorenz Books 2000

A Gardener's Guide to Orchids & Bromeliads
Sara Rittershausen, Merehurst 2000

Orchids for Everyone
Contributor Wilma Rittershausen
Salamander revised 1997

Propagating Plants (section on orchids)
Wilma Rittershausen
Dorling Kindersley 1999

Success with Orchids
Wilma Rittershausen
Smithmark 1997

The Orchid in Lore and Legend
Luigi Berliocchi
Timber Press 2000

The Manual of Cultivated Orchid Species
Phillip Cribb et al
Blandford

The Illustrated Encyclopedia of Orchids
Editor Alec Pridgeon
Timber 1992

Wild Orchids Across North America
A Botanical Travelogue
Phillip E. Keenan
Timber Press 1998

APPENDIX 4
VIDEOS ABOUT ORCHIDS

Potting the Burnham Way
Brian Rittershausen
Burnham 1993

Welcome to the World of Orchids
Brian and Sara Rittershausen
Burnham 1999

APPENDIX 5
SEEING AND BUYING ORCHIDS

A limited range of orchids is often on sale in larger garden centres and do-it-yourself superstores. They offer a reasonable introduction to orchid-growing, but you will need to look further afield for a wider variety and more information on orchid care and culture.

The best place to see and buy orchids is at one of the many orchid shows held each year. At these shows orchid plants are usually on sale as well as all sorts of orchid sundries, so there is the opportunity to see the plants in prime condition, ask the exhibitors for tips on how to grow them successfully, and make purchases.

The booklets and directories, available from the addresses given below are a good start for those wanting to find out where to see and buy orchids.

Britain
The British Orchid Growers' Association Growers and Buyers Guide
This free booklet which contains a list of orchid suppliers, orchid societies and orchid shows is available from:
Burnham Nurseries Ltd,
Forches Cross, Newton Abbot,
Devon TQ12 6PZ.

USA
The American Orchid Society Orchid Source Directory
This is the ultimate resource guide for the orchid hobbyist. It is available from:
The American Orchid Society,
16700 AOS Lane,
Del Ray Beach,
FL 33446-4350.

INDEX

Page numbers in *italics* refer to illustrations